PLANE SAFETY AND SURVIVAL

By Eric G. Anderson, M.D.

AERO PUBLISHERS, INC.
329 West Aviation Road, Fallbrook, CA 92028

Library of Congress No. 78-8247
ISBN 0-8168-7508-1 cloth
ISBN 0-8168-7510-3 paper

Library of Congress Cataloging in Publication Data

Anderson, Eric G
    Plane safety and survival.

        1. Survival (after air plane accidents, shipwrecks,
etc.) 2. Airplanes—Piloting. I. Title.
TL553.7.A53   629.132'52   78-8247
ISBN 0-8168-7508-1
ISBN 0-8168-7510-3 pbk.

Dedicated
to my wife Margaret
whose tolerant encouragement I quote . . .

"I don't mind your writing.
                    There are worse habits."

FOREWORD

Why this book? . . . and why by me?
I who
"will never now, it is too late
Master the art of flying straight.
Yet has — who knows so well as I?
A just sense of how not to fly."

ROBERT GRAVES
1958 1961 Co-Productions
Roturman, S.A.

Poet Graves' tribute *Flying Crooked* is, in fact, to a butterfly and yet as I flit here and there across our Nation and over varying types of terrain, perhaps some of what I learn as I sit at the foot of the masters can emerge to help others enjoy Flying the Outdoors.

E. G. Anderson
Derry, New Hampshire

ACKNOWLEDGMENTS - I

The author wishes to thank Dorothy Greenberg of Sports Car Press, Connecticut, for her encouragement; Annie Ashton, Librarian of the MacGregor Library, Derry, New Hampshire, for her help; and Carol Chase, Derry, New Hampshire, for her confidence that the punishment that she was being given at the typewriter was justified.

The kindness of Joe Christy, Editor of the Modern Aircraft Series in Lawton, Oklahoma, and Dave Mankus of Manchester, New Hampshire, is appreciated.

Acknowledgment is due Tom Bowen of Aero Publishers for his enthusiasm, a special thank you to Dora Reed for the careful consideration she gave the art layout of this book, and a much deserved tip of the hat to a great secretary, Marsha Laperriere.

ACKNOWLEDGMENTS - II

The following agencies and organizations are cordially thanked for their generosity in supplying photographs:

Alaska Travel Division, Dept. of Economic Development and Planning
Beech Aircraft Corporation
Burson-Marsteller
Cessna Aircraft Company
Colorado Travel Section
FAA Aviation News
Florida News Bureau Dept. of Commerce
Idaho Dept. of Commerce and Development
National Center for Atmospheric Research, Colorado
National Oceanic and Atmospheric Administration, Maryland
Nova Scotia Information Centre
Oregon State Highway Travel Section
Pennsylvania Bureau of Aviation, Department of Transportation
Piper Aircraft Corporation
Rocky Mountain National Park
South Dakota Dept. of Highways Travel Section
3 M Company
U. S. Coast Guard, First Coast Guard District, Boston
U.S. Dept. of Agriculture, Forest Service
U. S. Dept. of the Interior, National Park Service
Utah Travel Council
Vermont Agency of Development and Community Affairs
The Wilderness Society

Gratitude is also expressed to the various authors, writers, pilots and instructors quoted throughout this book.

Photo Credit/opposite page: Oregon State Highway Dept.

INTRODUCTION

"The most precious things in life are near
at hand, without money and without price"
John Burroughs
Born 1837   Catskill Mountains

INTRODUCTION

That Burroughs quote is still sometimes valid today but there is much to see in our life which is further afield, which introduces us to the light plane with costs proportional to the distance. In flying, a moment of hesitation, a chance consideration, an opportunity for improvement can alter the values received. The message of flying is the message of Life. . . first, know your enemies, learn who your friends are. Your enemies (and I'm sorry if this sounds like evangelism) are ignorance, sloth, indifference; and your friends (here goes the Pilgrim's Progress again) are skill, knowledge and comprehension. However, the skills for terrain flying are hard to accumulate now. You don't find them in the high hours airline captains isolated as they are in their pressurized cocoons above us, nor in the split reflex military pilots careering (if you'll excuse the pun) above, below and through us. No, the skills are scattered amongst some flight instructors, some mail pilots, the occasional FAA safety counselors, a few erudite magazine editors and flying organization writers. Without them, the book of aviation as it was painfully learned across our Nation in the 1920's and early 1930's would be forgotten and closed.

I have been self-critical that this book is so seldom in the air. It deals a lot with problems on the ground but in a way, once you have taken off, it makes little difference whether you are flying over a swamp, desert or a forest. The problems of the aerial portion of a journey are somewhat basic and once you have talked about wilderness flying over one kind of terrain, it is hard to think of something fresh to say about another. It is the ground portion that is so different, and those differences can be fatal.

I have not tried to make this a survival book although part of it has grown that way by itself. I have spent more time on mountain and overwater flying since they seem to be the two extremes. Perhaps if we understand them, we will know better the problems of the terrain between. We used to be taught as medical students . . . know diabetes, tuberculosis and syphilis and all other diseases will be made known unto you. If that is so, then know mountains and the sea . . .

Knowing how to survive is a lost art. Success depends on the attitude: "I'm going to live"—not—"I'm going to die." Training brings skill, and experience brings confidence. In August 1959, two pilots, Sheldon and Guerrera, crashed near Juneau, Alaska. They had filed a flight plan and knew they would be missed. They spent seven nights sharing one sleeping bag in turns. They expected rescue aircraft but had only one smoke torch. On the fifth day, an airplane flew over but too high for them to be sure they could be seen. They waited. On the seventh day, when a plane came over at a lower altitude, they fired their one torch, were spotted and later rescued. Such discipline, such common sense . . . maybe even such luck.

This book is written to help luck, to help you improve the odds. It is written for those in whom, as Zdenek Kopal says, "the cares of daily life have not blunted . . . interest . . . for leisure time to join a guided tour of the sky."

The ancient cultures of India believed that the world was simple, with the earth as flat as a tea tray, balanced on the backs of three elephants which themselves were supported on the shell of "a tortoise of universal proportions." Let's go fly and see if that is true.

And why fly? What's there to see? What's of interest? Only the world. Nigel

Calder's concept is fascinating. Since Mother Earth is 4600 million years old, he calls her "a lady of 46 megayears." He points out that the lady was arid for the first 45 years, that plants have appeared only in the last year, that the dinosaurs died eight months ago and that four hours ago, homo sapiens appeared. Fifteen minutes ago, Moses crossed the Red Sea, 10 minutes ago, Jesus was preaching and one minute ago, the Industrial Revolution began. At that speed, better get airborne before it is too late, before Life passes you by.

Well then, let's get this book in the air. It's fun to fly, so let's escape the pomposity of the printed word.

Let's go wilderness flying.

Fun flying comes from a comfortable familiarity with the aircraft, knowledge of its performance and awareness of its limitations.
Photo Credit: Piper Aircraft Corporation

TABLE OF CONTENTS

How to Fly, Enjoy and Survive Wilderness Areas and Remote Terrain

Photo Credit/opposite page:
National Center For Atmospheric Research, Colorado

1

WEATHER

WEATHER

A type of weather wisdom is necessary in flying remote areas. Not the glib, slick elegance of knowing how to read terminal forecasts, but rather the canny basic weather sagacity of the shepherd, the farmer and the outdoor woodsman. With perhaps added to that, a touch of the cautious, careful conservatism of the bank manager. It also doesn't hurt to have a bit of spare time, too, in order that you can say "I think I'll sit this one out," or as Richard Thomas the poet said more eloquently, "About face, before a tear can freeze against the wind."

Weather wisdom has been accumulated over the centuries. As far back as Matthew 16:3 we read, "And in the morning, it will be foul weather today: for the sky is red and lowring." Weather wisdom is also shown by the backwoodsman, for example Bill Riviere: "A sudden or surprise storm is almost as rare as a beaver with three-foot antlers," and by pilot weatherman Donald Morris: "The cloud with a Vmc remotely approaching that of the equipment you are flying . . . has yet to be spawned. Clouds do not really chase you."

Weather is the common denominator to any type of wilderness flying. Over water, the question is how does weather affect navigation; over mountains, how does terrain alter weather; in the desert, how does the pilot man stand up to the heat and in the frozen wastes, how does his machine the airplane stand up to the cold. Know weather and you understand terrain flying.

A certain amount of common sense and skepticism is necessary when weather forecasts are studied. I was reminded of the weakness of forecasting once in Texas when I had the wife of a weather forecaster in labor. Having examined the woman, the only patient in the Obstetrics Department, I came downstairs to tell the husband that it would be about a three-hour delay before he became a father. I was just telling him to go off for a cup of coffee when we both heard his baby crying upstairs. On my sheepish return, he said, "Boy, and they complain about weather forecasting!"

Let us look at what forecasters can do 12 hours in advance with accuracy of at least 75%.

(1) Passage of cold fronts or squall lines ± 2 hours.
(2) Passage of warm front or slow cold fronts ± 5 hours.
(3) Fast deepening of a low pressure area.
(4) Time of onset of a thunderstorm if radar available.
(5) Clearing of fog ± 2 hours.
(6) Rain ± 5 hours.
(7) Snow ± 5 hours.

However, the 12 hour in advance record drops to 50% accuracy for

(1) Turbulance.
(2) Heavy icing.
(3) Ceilings of 0-100 feet before they exist.
(4) Onset of thunderstorm not yet formed.
(5) Ice fog.
(6) Freezing rain.

Every pilot knows to update any weather information in his possession just prior to a flight, and the closer to his takeoff, the more accurate his data. If the pilot is going to go and take a look in marginal weather, he had better verify that he always has an out behind him and make his 180 in plenty of time and not before he has lost his alternate choice. I once circled for 40 minutes a pasture in the Catskill Mountains socked in by weather because the "shower" took its

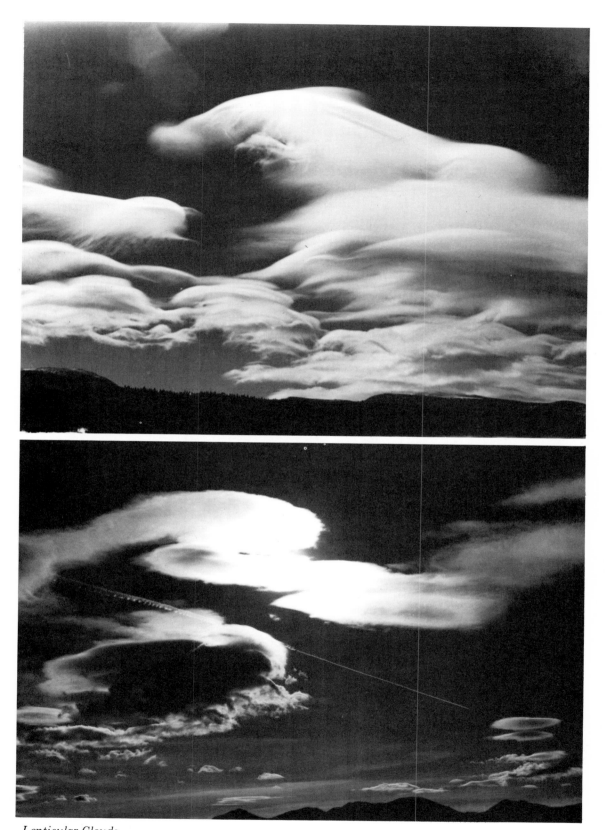

Lenticular Clouds
A sign of danger, lenticular (lens-shaped) clouds may come in many different forms even at times resembling sea horses or flying saucers. They are always a warning of the turbulence of the mountain wave.   *(Photo Credit: National Center for Atmospheric Research, Colorado)*

13

CLOUD GENERA

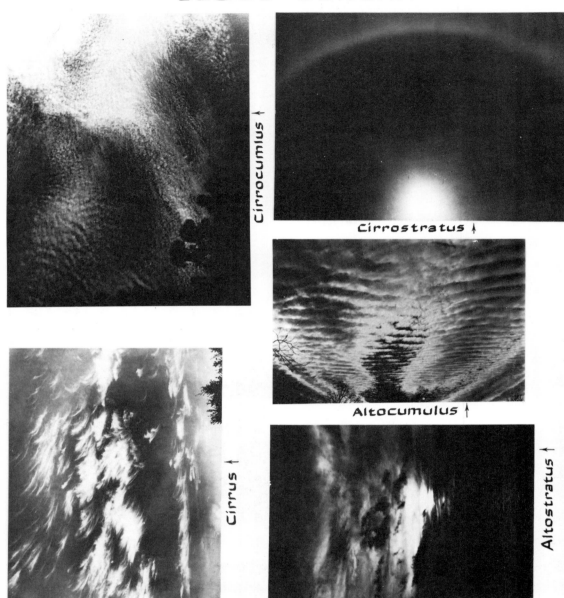

High Clouds 20,000 — 40,000 feet

(Bottom Left) Cirrus: *Thin feathery clouds in wisps — frequently first sign of a warm front, though small detached clouds can occur in Summer to signify fine weather. The significance of many of the clouds depends on the direction of the present wind.*

(Top Left) Cirrocumulus: *Thin glittering ice-crystal clouds. In early Summer morning, may be followed by afternoon thunderstorms.*

(Top Right) Cirrostratus: *Thin white sheets often forming halos and luminous circles around sun or moon. Usually in advance of warm front or behind cold front.*

Middle Clouds   7,000 - 20,000 feet

(Middle Right) Altocumulus: *Rounded rolls of white or gray — usually rain in 10-20 hours with squalls, gusts and thunderstorms.*

(Bottom Right) Altostratus: *More dense fibrous veils with sun dim as if through frosted glass.*

CLOUD GENERA

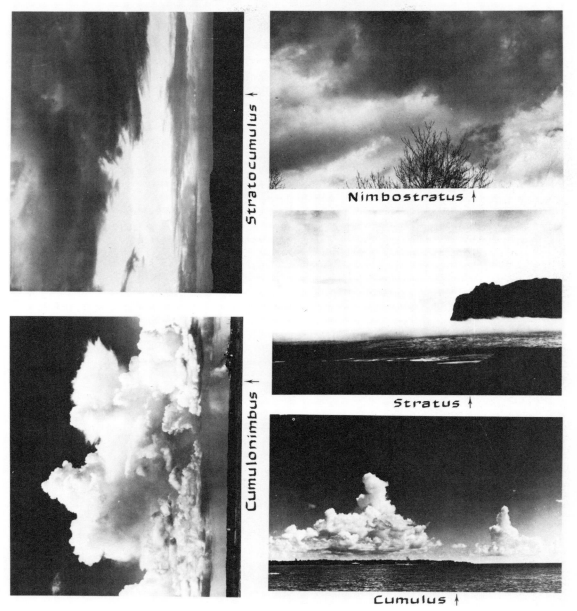

(Top Right) Nimbostratus: *Wet, thick, dark, shapeless rain or snow clouds. Rain may be continuous.*

Low Clouds   Ground to 8,000 feet

(Middle Right) Stratus: *A low uniform sheet like fog but not resting on the ground; smooth air; usually a sign of temperature inversion.*

(Top Left) Stratocumulus: *Soft gray rolls and masses — immediate harbingers of bad weather.*

Clouds of Vertical Development

(Bottom Right) Cumulus: *Dense, fluffy, cauliflower clouds, dome shaped tops and flat bases. May show fair weather if isolated and no vertical development.*

(Bottom Left) Cumulonimbus: *Towering, heavy masses often with anvil tops leveled by high winds. Tops may go to at least 60,000 feet visible 200 miles away. Rough, intense, turbulent, violent weather with snow or rain, squalls, thunderstorms and severe up and downdrafts.*

Photo Credit: National Oceanic and Atmospheric Administration)

time to pass. My concern was increased since in the back seat crouched a 75 pound German Shepherd dog that the veterinarian in the right hand seat and I were flying to Ohio for plastic surgery. I expected the dawg any moment to say, "Gee, can't you go around the other way for a change, I'm becoming airsick."

One observation I have about pilots is that we ask so many flying questions in our weather briefing but omit ones of great interest that we would ask were we not preoccupied pilots. For example, before checking any trip to a mountain area, the average camper would be interested in average day and night temperatures, the coldest and the warmest temperatures recorded, and the average wind velocity. He would want to know the percentages of days which were stormy in that area. He would consider the effect of altitude and wind chill, and have a composite picture of what to expect on an average day, then he would prepare and carry stores for slightly worse weather. How often do we glean such information for a flight into wilderness terrain?

Weather is considered in each chapter regarding different terrain but the reader is referred further to the following books:

Weather Flying
  (c) 1970 Robert Buck, MacMillan
Pilot's Weather Guide
  Modern Aircraft Series
Pilot's Handbook of Weather
  Aero Publishers
Aviation Weather
  FAA

Can we even estimate windspeed at ground level from the signs around us? The chart below clarifies this:

ESTIMATING WIND SPEED

Wind Velocity (mph)	Beaufort Scale	Air Movement	Indicators
0-1	0	Still	Smoke and steam rise straight up
2-3	1	Light air	Wind affects smoke direction but not waves
4-7	2	Slight breeze	You feel wind on face, leaves rustle, waves affected lightly, fresh snow eddies
8-12	3	Gentle breeze	Leaves and twigs move continuously
13-18	4	Moderate breeze	Small branches wave continuously, dust and snow stir
19-24	5	Fresh breeze	Whole small deciduous trees sway, tents flap
25-31	6	Strong breeze	Large branches wave, whitecaps on most waves
32-38	7	Moderate gale	Whole large trees sway
39-46	8	Fresh gale	Twigs break off, you have to lean into the wind in order to walk
47-54	9	Strong gale	Whole branches break off, high waves
55-63	10	Full gale	Poorly rooted trees topple, branches fly
64-72	11	Storm	Extensive wind damage of all types

Get the broad weather picture before any long cross country trip. Your TV set gives a useful initial briefing and weather trends can be seen by aerial viewing.

2
WILDERNESS MEDICINE

"Nolen, cut the crap. What do you want with fancy instruments? If you can't do this case with a rock and the top of a tin can, move over."
William A. Nolen, M.D.
The Making of A Surgeon (c) 1968
Random House

Coping with medical emergencies in the wilderness is a lot easier than handling emergencies in flight. There is almost always time to assess a situation in medicine before action is required. When I see ambulances screaming through cities, I often reflect, as they jeopardize bystanders and other drivers, how seldom the extra minute makes any difference. A small booklet on first aid is invaluable and can be studied with the patient and the problem in front of you. I had a doctor friend who, newly qualified, would on house calls always ask the housewife if he could use her rest room after he had examined the patient. There, in privacy, he would stand and study his handbook on diseases before flushing the toilet as his alibi and returning to prescribe.

The golden rules as a first aider in the outback are similar to those for doctors. First, do no harm; stop bleeding; verify that the patient can breathe properly; rest any injured part; be patient and give nature a chance to heal.

MEDICAL PROBLEMS FOR THE OUTDOOR PILOT

Since I have more hours doctoring than flying, this should be the easiest chapter to talk about, but my problem is what to leave out (got it, I'll omit the diseases I don't understand.).

Wilderness medicine, like good survival, starts at home with adequate consideration being given to any health problem of any of the flyers. Some people really should stay home. I am constantly astounded in our hospital Emergency Room by some problem patients who

COMFORT STATION
A pilot should consider his crew's needs. Clockwise bottom right: alcohol sponges, wash-ups, sunglasses, hats, Kleenex, coffee can with lid as urinal, liquid soap, chewing gum and nasal spray.
Photo Credit: E. G. Anderson

clearly should have stayed home and not ventured into another environment and I live in a small New Hampshire town, not a wilderness (although people in New Jersey might dispute that). People with serious heart, lung or kidney problems should not fly into situations where they can be days away from proper medical care.

I think the easiest way is to consider how the outdoors pilot is affected by

(1) Insults of Weather and Nature

HEAT

Sunburn: Most of us know our susceptibility which depends on amount of pigmentation and previous tanning. Whether we burn depends on the intensity of the solar radiation which is greater in the clearer high altitudes and intensified by reflection off water, snow and rocks. This reflection can even give you a painful burn below your chin and in your nostrils. A broad brimmed hat, a neckerchief and black engine oil, charcoal or mud below your eyes can prevent this to a degree in survival situations. Chapsticks for lips can be effective. Screening agents can be used at altitudes, like Sea and Ski, Solbar and Coppertone; but those who really suffer should smear on thick zinc oxide cream like Zincofax. Aspirin and cold compresses will help too.

Aspirin, incidentally, is a miracle drug. When doctors on T.V. guest shows are asked what one drug they would take to a desert island, the answer always is aspirin. Aspirin reduces swelling even where patients have no pain.

Dehydration: Dehydration is caused by the increased water loss with the increased sweat output of the active outdoorsman and moisture loss due to faster breathing. At altitude, the air is dryer too, and people do not remember to drink enough even when water supply is unlimited. The delicate balance of heat made and heat lost is upset. Salt tablets 0.5 gram can be bought over-the-counter. The usual dose in hot climates is two tablets four times a day but a half teaspoon of salt in a glass of water may be better tolerated than a tablet.

Heat Exhaustion occurs as a minor nuisance after prolonged activity in heat. Essentially, the body succeeds in cooling itself by opening up blood vessels in the skin and sweating. The heat exhausted patient still has an efficient mechanism of sweating. He will be faint, with a fast pulse, nausea and a normal temperature. His skin will be cold and clammy. The treatment is to lie down and rest with the feet up; take cold drinks; go on *slowly* once pulse and respiration rate is normal.

Heat Stroke (Sunstroke) is a step further on; the body's efficiency has been lost and the person overwhelmed. The skin is not sweating. It is flushed, hot and dry; the temperature is 105 degrees. The patient here is more ill and should be cooled fast. Cold wet compresses, alcohol baths, blowing on the skin will all help. Limbs should be massaged. Seek a place of shade. A person newly recovered from sunstroke cannot then go on like a heat exhaustian patient. Moral—wear a hat, use shade, drink plenty and go canny in hot weather.

COLD

Hypothermia: As any outdoorsman knows, still dry cold is acceptable but wet windy cold is not. People ski in bathing suits in some locales because of absence of wind. There is a definite relationship to wind and temperature equivalent, and most readers are familiar with the wind chill table (see Frozen Terrain Flying). Illness associated with cold, fatigue and exposure is called hypothermia and is responsible for many outdoor deaths each year. Poor consideration to clothing plays a part in this problem. Gene Fear, Chairman of the President's Council on Mountain Safety, has said, "If we could just get the jeans off them, we could save a lot of lives." Jeans are useless as cold weather clothing. Wool is ideal as it still insulates, even when wet; normally, wet clothing increases chilling by conducting heat away from the body up to 240 times faster. Contact with cold objects such as sitting on cold rocks also causes heat loss. Windblow further intensifies the problem and there have been hypothermia deaths on ocean beaches with temperatures of 50 degrees F. Radiation is the greatest cause of heat loss and an unprotected head can lose 50% of the body's heat production at 40 degrees F, and the weatherwise say, "If your feet are cold, put on your hat." To prevent heat loss, your clothing can be augmented in survival situations by padding below your shirt with dried grass, moss, paper or even the stuffing from the airplane seats. If heat loss is excessive in a hostile environment, death can occur in three hours without shelter.

The initial symptom of hypothermia is shivering, which if intense is a sign that the body temperature is down at least 3 degrees, and that the person needs to be treated. The patient then becomes uncoordinated and incapable of significant muscular effort; thinking becomes slow and ponderous (as in those who write books) giving rise to poor judgment, and muscular rigidity changes imperceptibly into semicoma and collapse.

Hypothermia is treated by preventing further loss by shelter, sleeping bag and warm dry clothing, and by increasing heat production by hot foods and liquids, lighting a fire and exercising. To be prevented,

you must be aware of the problem and keep its possibility in mind, and that means sensible clothes, eating regularly and carrying shelter as you go. Anything is better than nothing—a simple sheet of plastic is valuable. I recall how welcome a simple plastic gas cape was in field maneuvers in the Army for nights spent huddled in trenches and frozen ditches. Stop early on the trail if any of the party seems chilled and once stopped, keep the party exercising building shelter and chopping wood. Avoid alcohol as it warms the extremities and thereafter chills the body. If you are winter camping, the tent can present problems. If completely water tight, the pint of water vapor exhaled by each camper will condense on the inside of the roof and wet the inhabitants. The answer is a plastic fly sheet with an air space between it and a non-waterproof tent. A foam or rubber mattress insulates better than air mattresses and sleeping bags should be down or a synthetic, like Dupont Fiberfill II. Remember how Baden-Powell, the founder of the Boy Scouts, used to insist that his campers have more blankets below than above. Anyone who has felt the wretched cold seeping and creeping into his bones from frozen ground does not have to be reminded of that.

Frost Bite is another problem of cold weather, and is more common than some Southerners realize. My first New England winter after four years in Texas saw me digging out a car in a snowstorm after a house call. I felt no pain in my ear, but later a small piece of it dropped off—thought I was going to look like Van Gogh.

Predisposing factors in frostbite are overexertion, sweating, dehydration, fatigue and lack of food. The symptoms are coldness and numbness in the extremity. Usually feet, hands, ears and nose go in that order. The part which is injured then starts to feel warm although the skin becomes yellow and hard.

The treatment is to rewarm rapidly by gentle means but for deep frostbite, don't thaw the part unless you can keep it warm thereafter. The best method is warm water at 110 degrees F for about 30 minutes. Avoid rough massage. Don't warm slowly or by rubbing with snow and don't exercise the injured part or overheat it. Give aspirin, warm food and drinks but avoid alcohol and tobacco.

Trench Foot: Another cold wet weather problem is trench foot, which my father once described to me graphically from his years at the Front in World War I. It develops slowly and can be prevented by attempting to give immersed feet a chance to dry off and warm up at times (see Swamp Flying).

Snow Blindness also can be mentioned here. It develops about six hours after exposure with the eyes feeling scratchy, as if sand had entered them. Such feelings are also experienced with allergies. Blinking then becomes painful and the eyes get puffy and red. The experience can be frightening and sufferers have even had to be blindfolded at times. Usually cold compresses help. The problem can be prevented by sunglasses, with the wrap around kind being more useful, but you can improvise with a sheet of cardboard, birch bark or even a dollar bill into which you have cut slits.

Mountain or Altitude Sickness needs discussion. Minor symptoms can occur at 7,000 feet mean sea level but most cases happen above 10,000 feet. The first symptom is often loss of appetite and slight headache, then there is a feeling of apathy and general malaise. The periphery of the body may then look a little dusky or blue; for example, the earlobes, fingertips and lips. If in doubt, compare the patient's nails with those of the rest of the party. A dry cough may ensue with palpitations, dizziness, shortness of breath, nausea and vomiting. The spit may be frothy and blood stained. The remedy is to get the patient down to a lower altitude fast as even 2,000 feet can make a difference. If you are at a high altitude airfield and have oxygen in the plane, give the patient a whiff of that.

Before we leave the weather, let us look at a few ways that our enemies of the skies can hurt us on the ground. Lightning kills about 150-400 Americans a year and injures 250-1,000 depending on whose figures you rely. That total is certainly greater than deaths from tornados and hurricanes combined. In Texas, I was impressed when asking new patients for their family history to note how often a relative had been killed by lightning. The distance in miles that you are from a thunderstorm is found by noting the flash, counting the seconds until you hear the rumble of thunder, then dividing that number by five. For instance, five seconds to the sound means the storm is one mile away. I see that Florida has about 80 thunderstorms a year which travel over the ground with an average speed of 20 knots (range 5-50 knots). You are more likely to be struck at the beginning of a storm, hence the name "bolt from the blue." Don't run for the nearest tree or any high ground. Get off peaks and ridges and don't be the tallest object in an open field. Keep clear of metal as many have been killed holding fishing rods, umbrellas or golf clubs. Try to get low in a ravine, ditch or deep cave, or even make a fox hole. If in water, get out as you are in great danger since water is an excellent conductor. Bolts hitting the surface will electrocute for hundreds of feet. The charge is not retained by the victim, who may safely be touched. His chances of survival if struck are about 50-50 and the patient requires cardiopulmonary resuscitation (CPR), just as if he had had a heart attack.

Tornados are more common. It is said that in Kansas, every person is in a tornado danger zone at least once a year. In Mississippi, you have one chance in 100 in your lifetime of being injured in a tornado but only 10,000 deaths have occurred in the United States in the last 50 years. April, May and June see half the cases, with 80% occurring in the afternoon— which is another reason for the early start in light plane vacationing. Winds of 500 miles per hour have been recorded in the 1,000 foot wide track of tornados, although their speed of travel is usually about 40 miles per hour in the 10 to 40 mile long blitz they give to the earth.

(2) Insults by Other Creatures and Pests

Here, we are not attacking Don Rickles, but rather what the French Canadian National Parks call guerre aux insectes. They produce a little pamphlet giving useful tips. Loose fitting, tightly woven clothing with long sleeves and pants tucked into socks helps to reduce the area of risk. Avoid dark colors since this seems to attract insects. Avoid perfumed shampoos and scented soaps; use repellents and apply to skin and clothing. The best repellents contain Diethyl Toluamide; e.g., Off, 6-12, Cutter. Use smoke and wind as a means of keeping insects off and avoid wet areas such as forests, marshes and stagnant water.

MOSQUITOES: They are most active at night, in shade areas and on dull overcast days. The male is a vegetarian and it is the female who is the bloodsucker as she needs protein for her eggs. Head nets may be required.

BLACKFLIES arrive later in the spring and last until July. They bite only during the day, preferring sunrise and sunset. They like shaded areas of exposed skin. Hat rims, therefore, seem to attract, and every May in New Hampshire we see patients with huge glands in the back of their neck from blackfly bites of the scalp.

HORSEFLIES and DEERFLIES are more difficult to discuss. Insect repellents are not so effective and those very aggressive larger insects are frequently found around cattle.

CATERPILLARS have hairs with blistering secretions. I have treated many small children who collected them as pets!

CHIGGERS and ITCH MITES are small, about 1/200th of an inch long, and lie in long grass and brush to get onto campers' legs. Diethyl Toluamide will repel as will sulphur, and Kwell ointment can be used to kill the parasites that get onto your body, but try not to scratch as they can cause tattooing.

TICKS are larger, about 1/8th of an inch, and can cause tick bite fever and Rocky Mountain Spotted Fever. They also cause an odd phenomenon called tick bite paralysis, a reversible state once the tick is removed. The treatment is to pair off (m m m!) and inspect each other's body twice a day. You can remove them with tweezers or a pin, or make them back off by covering with vaseline which shuts off their air as does alcohol and kerosene. A hot cigarette butt may make them let go. If the head is left behind in your skin, scratch the area out with a needle daily. Check out your dog.

BEES and associated insects like wasp, yellow jacket and hornet belong to the order called Hymenoptera. 2% of the population have some allergy to those and their situation should be clarified before such people become flying campers. 50% of all deaths from venomous bites are from this order. In Texas, we used to think that many of the "heart attack" deaths in the woods were probably due to insect bite allergy. The treatment is ice or cold compresses and antihistamines. Severe reactions are beyond the scope of this book.

BLACK WIDOW SPIDERS cause exaggerated reports and legends. 95% of those bitten survive but 6 die each year in the United States. The spiders prowl around wood piles, ghost towns, dumps and outdoor buildings and toilets. My first patient with this problem was bitten on his genitals as he sat on the outside john and he had such a rigid abdomen that I thought he had perforated a duodenal ulcer initially.

TARANTULA SPIDERS look fierce but, in fact, are not really a problem for man. We sometimes see bites from the Brown Recluse Spider and once I had a woman patient with such a bite on her chest that about half of her breast rotted away and she was very ill.

SCORPIONS also have a bit of mystique to them, but only two out of 40 species are poisonous . . . the other 38 cause only swelling, pain and discoloration. There were only eight deaths in a ten-year period; six in Arizona and two in Texas. Park Rangers scoff at the old wives tale of shaking out boots and sleeping bags, but do it themselves nevertheless. They are nocturnal creatures. I used to go back to my office in Texas in the evening to catch up with dictation until I saw how the old ground floor building was invaded each night by those beasts.

RABID ANIMALS are on the increase, and 30,000 people a year in the United States have to take a course of rabies shots—five die of this disease each year. Common infected creatures are skunks, foxes and bats. You may not need to be bitten, and in 1968 Texas and New Mexico researchers found when two scientists died that perhaps droplet inhaled infection from bat caves had caused the problem. The prevention is: don't touch dead animals, don't hand feed wild animals and avoid nocturnal prowlers if they come out in the daytime or appear to lose their fear of man, as this may be a sign of the disease. Remember, even if the animal is not rabid, the bite can cause tetanus or other infection.

SNAKE BITE is almost a subject all on its own.

In the United States, there are 45.000 bites a year with 75% of the bites being on the legs (hence the value of cowboy boots). Probably 8,000 of those bites are venomous but over a five-year study of 550 cases, there were only 12 deaths annually in the United States. (Russell et al, Snake Venom Poisoning, JAMA, 233, 341-344, 1975). Many of those who died had pre-existing conditions and it has been said that more die in their bathtubs in the United States than from snake bite. In the world, there are 3,000 species of snakes with only 10% being a danger to man. In the United States, there are 120 species of snakes of which 20 are venomous. Four snakes are a problem in the USA, namely: the coral snake and the three members of the pit viper, copperhead, cottonmouth (water mocassin) and rattlesnake. Although there are differences amongst each snake species, some general theories can be stated.

Don't provoke snakes; even the non-aggressive ones may choose to retaliate as snakes "break all rules and can't be trusted." Don't poke in holes. Don't step blindly over logs or high grass—in fact, in snake country, many outdoorsmen would go around rather than over. Don't disturb rocks or fuss with your environment in the outdoors. I had a Forestry Service patient once in Texas who brushed below him as he sat down on a log. He felt a sting on his finger like a briar scratch. He turned around and put his hand back in the same position to see where the thorn was and the coral snake bit him again. This was the only time I had a snake bite case in the office where the patient's friends were still laughing although the man ultimately nearly lost his finger.

If you come face to face with a snake, back away; after all what are you trying to prove? If you are five feet from the snake, you are outside its striking range as no reptile can strike more than two-thirds its length. What about being chased by one—we've all heard the tall tale of the man on horseback at gallop overtaken by a mean rattlesnake. Well, the fastest snake, the sidewinder, covers 4.4 feet per second and normal walking gait is 5.8 feet per second.

What about the other adage: "Dangerous even when dead." This one is true. Their hearts will beat for two days in decapitated bodies and there are reflex motions in the snake which will enable the head to bite a stick if poked by it for many minutes. One severed head was biting by reflex action for one hour. Thus, the ruling—don't pick up dead snakes.

The four American snakes of importance are:
(1) THE CORAL SNAKE
    This is not aggressive but is very dangerous. It has short fangs and a small mouth and cannot bite large objects. Its poison, volume for volume, is very powerful and the only redeeming feature is that sometimes only a little venom is injected. It is about 20-30 inches long and is recognized by red, yellow and black bands where the red and yellow are adjacent, which distinguishes this snake from serpents where the red yellow is not contiguous.
(2) The PIT VIPERS are divided into:
    a. COPPERHEAD, which is the next largest poisonous snake.

It measures 24-36 inches and has a coppery red head with an hourglass pattern. It is said that this snake has bitten more people in the United States than any other, but fortunately the bites are not usually significant.

    b. COTTONMOUTH. This snake, 30-48 inches long, is much more aggressive and will stand its ground. It is a dark color with a white open mouth, hence its name. An aquatic serpent, it is sometimes called the water mocassin. Those snakes are much more dangerous and seeing one at my feet once in Texas when I was fishing almost made me lay an egg, especially since I was standing on its semisubmerged log in my bare feet.

    c. RATTLESNAKES go from 15-72 inches long and inhabit a variety of locations. They are quite unpredictable but the larger ones are more aggressive. They are relatively deaf with poor eyesight but are very sensitive to heat, smell and vibrations. Their feeding time is usually two hours before and after sunset. Their diet is mostly small mammals and outdoor pilots. They tolerate temperature change poorly. At 65 degrees F, they barely move; 80-90 degrees is their best range; they become unwell above 100 degrees and die of heat stroke if *their* temperature goes above 110 degrees F.

You'll notice I've been dragging my heels on treatment, the reason being that the subject is controversial. Various authorities differ on the subject of ice, tourniquet and cutting with suction. Let us consider a snake bite in sequence: Ouch! Bitten! Can we identify the snake or even kill it for later study? What size was it? The patient lies down and the attendant reassures him, "No sweat—I've read old Anderson's book!" There is no need to cut and suck if the snake was small, if the bite was on an extremity and if you can be at a doctor's office in one-half to one hour. On the other hand, if the bite was on the face, neck or trunk or if the snake was more than 3½ feet long and you are out in the boonies, you should cut and suck. A venous tourniquet is applied if a limb was bitten and two small cuts are made—not crosswise—but longwise on the limb:

INCISIONS FOR SNAKE BITE

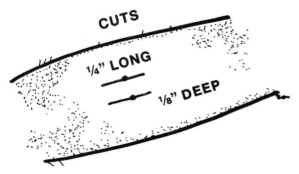

You can use a razor blade or a scalpel for this. Turn your back to the patient and conceal your hand (y'know, be a real sneaky doctor), then either use a rubber suction device or suck the cuts by mouth. Do not use your mouth if you have ulcers or canker sores in your mouth. Spit out the sucked material. If you will have the patient at a doctor within an hour, don't use ice; otherwise, a cool compress should be applied to the bite. Don't pack or freeze the part in ice as this just adds to tissue injury and tissue death.

Children do badly because they panic, get their circulation excited which spreads the venom, and because they are small size, which means a relatively high dose of the injected poison. Keep the patient calm—he should be carried or walked slowly to a doctor. Don't run. I once had a patient with a little tough 105-pound mother who carried her 12-year-old boy four miles on her back when he was bitten by a cottonmouth because she knew the importance of resting the patient.

The final treatment is antivenin, which is produced by Wyeth Laboratories and keeps for five years. Any constant traveller in snake country might want to carry his own and discuss this with his doctor. A simple Cut and Suck Kit put out by Cutter also should be carried.

Other snake bite points to be remembered (which means I forgot to put them in at the appropriate places) are that suction should be continued for the first hour and that use of tourniquet should be intermittent; e.g. release for 90 seconds every 10 minutes. The tourniquet should be as tight as when a lab technician takes a blood specimen from you, but not so tight that your hand goes white and you lose your pulse at the wrist. The patient may get worse each time you release the tourniquet but you have no choice, and in fact, may have to keep putting it on higher and higher as the swelling advances up the limb.

GILA MONSTER bites are not common, although in 1577 the Spanish explorer Francisco Hernandez found the bite painful and poisonous but not fatal. The small 20-inch lizard is protected by law and seems to know it. It doesn't hang on tightly and can be pulled off by force. Use ice and rest the part.

PLANT PESTS mostly mean the poison ivy type of problem. Poison oak out West, poison sumac in the

Southeast and poison ivy in the Central and the Northeast may also be found elsewhere. They all produce an identical oleoresin. Wash the part with soap and water; if possible have a shower and shampoo and change your clothing. Some cortisone tablets and cream should be carried in anticipation by susceptible persons.

(3) Illness in the Outdoors

CONSTIPATION is due to the relative dehydration and reduced fluid intake of the traveller. He also is not getting as much bulk diet as at home (fruit and salads, etc.). Treat by increasing fluid intake. In survival situations, you may have to grease your finger with Vaseline or animal fat and use it to lubricate your rectum.

DIARRHEA may be the "traveller's trots" from new bugs you have picked up or germs from inadequately washed food. You may wish to carry some Lomotil tablets with you. With diarrhea and food poisoning, it is important to replace fluids and usually clear fluids are tolerated. A broad spectrum antibiotic like Ampicillin may be required.

HEART ATTACKS can occur due to the strain of altitude, exercise or just from chance. Any patient with chest pain or collapse should be seen in the nearest emergency room. Probably any busy outdoor traveller should take a course from a Red Cross training group.

(4) Accidents

ABRASIONS usually respond to washing with soap and application of a simple antibiotic cream like Neosporin. Don't overuse band-aids—allow wounds to breathe. It's an unusual wound that needs a band-aid on it through the night.

CONTUSIONS or bruises should be treated with ice or cold compresses initially and an ace bandage. The idea is to stop swelling by using ice for the first 24-36 hours, then to use hot packs thereafter to encourage a richer blood supply to the part to speed healing.

FRACTURES are almost beyond the scope of this book. There are, however, some general rules. Bones on which you stand, i.e., weight bearing, require at least six to eight weeks to heal. If in doubt, be generous. Non weight bearing bones are less of a problem and can be expected to do better. Broken bones, if deformed, need to be realigned, but the body has great power to remodel bones, and immobilization of a part may be all that is necessary. Buy a few plaster of Paris bandages for your first aid kit in case you do not have natural materials for splinting. You can splint an injured part to the rest of the body; ror example, fasten an arm to the torso with an ace bandage, or a bad leg to a good leg, or a finger to a neighboring finger with Scotch tape.

SPECIFIC AREAS:

LEG: If the toe looks crooked, pull on it, then splint to the toe next door. This also refers to fingers. The ankle is often sprained and requires rest and elevation for several days. If the bone protuberances on either side of the ankle are very tender to even gentle pressure, this is suggestive of fracture. If the area below those bumps is tender, this implies ligament injury not bone injury. Ankle sprains can be strapped by adhesive tape or ace bandage.

ARM: In contrast to the ankle, sprains of the wrist are rare and injury there usually means fracture.

SHOULDER is easily dislocated and usually readily fixed by lying alongside the patient with your stockinged foot in his armpit. You then pull gently and move your toe outwards.

RIBS can be strapped with an ace bandage for comfort.

For useful information, the reader is referred to:

(1) The free pamphlet on Wilderness

Medicine by John Blosser, M.D. Portland Oregon Clinic and Sierra Club brochure obtained from the magazine *Emergency Medicine*, Fischer-Murray, Inc., 280 Madison Avenue, New York, NY 10016.

(2) First Aid Chart can be obtained free from the Metropolitan Life Insurance Company, Health and Welfare Division, One Madison Avenue, New York, NY 10010.

(3) The local chapter of the American Heart Association or Red Cross.

BURNS: Apply cold water, cut away clothing, use Telfa dry dressing and bandage. Give aspirin. Estimate extent of surface area involved and expect shock if this is more than 30%.

LACERATIONS (Cuts): If they gape widely or continue to bleed, they need stitching which is very easy. Ask your family doctor for a few suture kits if you are going to be far from civilization; there are now disposable kits which he can buy for you.

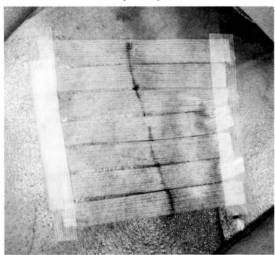

Mylar sterile adhesive tapes are superior to Band Aids and "butterflies" and quite satisfactory for closing many cuts.   Photo Credit: 3M Company

FISH HOOKS SKIN: Push all the way through with pliers, then cut off the barb and retract.

GUNSHOT WOUNDS: Apply iodine or disinfectant. Apply a big gauze pad— cover with ace. Don't dig for bullet. See doctor.

BLISTERS: Cover with a Band-Aid from which you have removed the pad. This supports the skin and is usually adequate.

SPLINTERS are common. Have fine tweezers called splinter forceps or dig with a needle or a fine scalpel blade. Below the nail, cut a V shape in the nail to expose the splinter, then remove.

ATHLETE'S FOOT: Keep dry. Use talc or medicated powder like Desenex.

FOREIGN BODY IN THE EYE is a painful situation. Use local anesthetic drops Ophthaine to make the eye numb and then try to get the foreign body off cornea with a Q-tip. Have a good light and a steady hand. Stop if it is too difficult. Turn back upper eyelid to exclude foreign bodies on the upper conjunctiva. Wash out copiously, then use boric acid eyewash or an eye antibiotic. See doctor if foreign body persists.

Printed below is

CARDIOPULMONARY RESUSCITATION as demonstrated on a small card obtained free from the American Heart Association.

CPR
IN BASIC LIFE SUPPORT
Place victim flat on his back on a hard surface.
If unconscious, open airway.

Neck lift, head tilt **or** Chin lift, head tilt

1

2 **If not breathing, begin artificial breathing.**
4 quick full breaths.
If airway is blocked,
try back blows, abdominal or
chest thrusts and finger probe
until airway is open.

3 **Check carotid pulse.**

4 **If pulse absent, begin artificial circulation.** Depress sternum 1½" to 2".

One Rescuer	Two Rescuers
15 compressions	5 compressions
rate 80 per min.	rate 60 per min.
2 quick breaths	1 breath

CONTINUE UNINTERRUPTED UNTIL
ADVANCED LIFE SUPPORT IS AVAILABLE

© 1978 American Heart Association

Finally, CARBON MONOXIDE POISONING: Watch for it in winter flying of old aircraft especially, in cooking in confined spaces and in situations like snow caves.

FIRST AID FOR THE FAMILY
(Hints from Metropolitan Life)

Learn what to do in an emergency. Take a first aid training course. Planning and preparing now may help save a life later. Use these directions as brief reminders.

ASPHYXIATION (breathing stopped): Get the patient to fresh air. Call physician. Start ABC of life support.

BITES, ANIMAL: Wash wounds with soap under running water. Have animal caught alive, if possible, so that it can be tested for rabies. Take patient to physician.

BLEEDING: Press hard with sterile compress directly over wound until bleeding stops. If bleeding is severe, call physician.

MINOR CUTS — Wash with soap under warm running water. Apply sterile compress.

SEVERE NOSEBLEED — Keep patient quiet and seated with head tilted back. Firmly pinch lower part of nose for at least 4-5 minutes while patient breathes through mouth, or pack bleeding nostril with cotton and pinch. If bleeding does not stop, call physician.

BURNS: MILD (skin unbroken-no blisters) — Immerse burned area in cold water or apply towels soaked in ice water.

SEVERE — Call physician. Apply sterile compresses. Do not break blisters or try to clean burn. Keep patient quiet and comfortably warm.

IF CAUSED BY CHEMICALS — Wash area very thoroughly with water. Call physician.

CHOKING (foreign body in throat or windpipe): Do nothing momentarily. Give the cough reflex time to work. Back slapping or reaching into the mouth with a finger may force the object down into the windpipe. Cough spasms will usually expel the object. *Only as a last resort:* If chocking continues and the patient becomes increasingly blue, then slap the back sharply between the shoulder blades. If breathing stops, start mouth-to-mouth rescue breathing. Call physician and rush the person to hospital.

CONVULSIONS: Be sure that patient is where he can't hurt himself. Push away nearby hard objects. Loosen clothing around neck. If possible, put thick wad of cotton between his teeth so that he doesn't bite his tongue. When convulsions stop, turn head to side. If convulsions do not stop by themselves, sponge patient's head and neck with cool water. Call physician.

ELECTRIC SHOCK: Turn off electric power if possible. Do not touch patient until contact is broken. Pull him from contact using rope, wooden pole, or loop of dry cloth. If breathing has stopped, start ABC of life support. Call physician.

EYE, CHEMICALS IN: Have patient lie down at once. Pour cupfuls of water immediately into inner corner of eye until chemical is thoroughly removed. Cover with sterile compress. Call physician.

FAINTING: If patient feels faint, seat him and lower head to knees. If he becomes unconscious, lay him down with head turned to the side. Loosen clothing. See that lots of fresh air reaches him. Do not give liquids. Wave smelling salts or aromatic spirits of ammonia under nose. After consciousness returns, keep patient lying quiet for at least 15 minutes. If faint lasts for more than a few minutes, call physician.

FALLS: Stop any severe bleeding and cover wounds with sterile dressing. Keep patient warm and comfortable. If a broken bone is suspected, do not move patient unless absolutely necessary (as in case of fire, for example). If patient has continued pain, call physician.

POISONING (by mouth): Call physician. If container is available, use antidote recommended on label. If patient is conscious, induce vomiting, EXCEPT FOR LYE, OTHER CAUSTICS, AND PETROLEUM PRODUCTS. If antidote or poison is unknown, give fluid in large amounts.

STINGS, INSECT: Remove "stinger," if possible, and apply solution of ammonia and water, or paste of baking soda. In case of unusual swelling or collapse, consult physician immediately. Allergic persons should prevent recurrence of severe reaction by receiving desensitization treatment from physician.

UNCONSCIOUSNESS: If there is no danger of fracture, turn patient on side so that secretions may drain from mouth. Keep him warm. Call physician. If patient stops breathing, start ABC of life support. Never give an unconscious person food or liquid.

Lava, tall pine trees and glacier-fed streams place this scene in Oregon's Three Sisters Wilderness Area west of Bend. This area is a virtual paradise for hikers, climbers, pack-campers, photographers and naturalists. Family campers, boaters, fishermen and picnickers are accommodated on the fringes of the primitive region, where centuries ago great mountain peaks showered streams of molten lava. Mt. Bachelor rises 9,060 feet in the background. (Oregon State Highway Department)

3
CAMPING
BY
PLANE

*"Rough realities in a life . . .
take the poetry out of the visions of joy,
peace, contentment and success."*
                                    H. W. Wiley

CAMPING BY PLANE

Introduction

Gear
     Shelter
     Clothing
     Cookware
     Food
     Water Purifying
     Other Equipment

Skills
     Fire Starting
     Cooking With Minimal Gear
     Laying Out the Camp
     Planning the Vacation

CAMPING BY PLANE

As I thumb through the endless lists of flying organizations; The Flying Fools, The Flying Spelunkers, The Flying Submariners, The Flying Acrophobiacs and so on, I am struck by the absence of any Flying Campers Organization. Never were two interests more mutually suited. The absence of a good directory of grass strips and nearby attractions across America is a surprising omission.

You can't take your favorite mechanic with you, but you can get routine service done before you go, rather than en route. Photo Credit: E. G. Anderson

What a difference it makes to long cross country vacations if some of the hassle of ground transportation is avoided. The family which cannot set up an adequate overnight camp at the end of the day in less time than waiting for a downtown motel ride is woefully undertrained. To me, plane camping is plain camping. You don't need lots of equipment—remember Thoreau, "a man is rich in proportion to what he can do without," and Charles Jansen says, "gain more with less." Travel light because the name of the game is keep the weight down, and all flying campers benefit by the backpacker revolution which has brought so many inexpensive, lightweight items to your nearby shopping center. I feel, too, that if you have to lug around a heavy reference book of campsites, you have missed the point of plane camping or maybe your friendly

Polishing your bird really does add a few knots and cleaning the windshield makes all the difference if you're a shutterbug. Photo Credit: E. G. Anderson

neighborhood FBO has. Camping by plane, to me, is setting up your tent in or within walking distance of an airstrip. *The AOPA Directory of Airports* and a sectional map covering your destination becomes more useful than any campsite listing. Omigosh, I can feel your incensed hot breath on the back of my neck: "You call that camping!" and so on. Answer: "Yup—I camp to fly, not fly to camp." To be fair, however, I can think of some occasions where the plane was tied down in an open clearing and the magic of the vacation was in the solitude and privacy of the lonely campsite and communion with Nature.

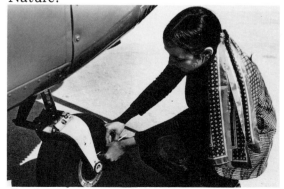

For long cross countries, a tire gauge is a most useful but underutilized tool. Do you know right now the correct tire pressure for your plane?
Photo Credit: E. G. Anderson

For plane camping, the FBO and airport manager become very important persons. I have never found them unreasonable and have camped both in small grass strips miles from cities and on the grass in a corner of huge airfields which boasted the name "International Airport." Maybe I did that to prove something but, my God—the noise. I remember, too, once in a big airport in Michigan, being told that the "Snow Goose" would be landing at midnight and might disturb us with its noise. It didn't, but my small son woke me every bloody hour to ask if the "Snow Goose" had landed yet.

Camping allows you to feel you can handle wilderness. It makes you more aware of Nature and considerate of the needs of others who enjoy the outdoor life. I don't think that those who buzz National Parks and intrude on the tranquility of others can be campers or outdoor lovers. Come on, you know what I mean . . . I mean OUTDOOR lovers not outdoor LOVERS. Richard Frisbie, author of *It's a Wise Woodsman Who Knows What's Biting Him* (c) 1969 Doubleday, says we are soft and require restrooms and modern facilities everywhere we go. He states we follow the trail not of "explorers and mountain men, but of plumbers. Lewis and Clark? Isn't that a construction firm?" Let's prove him wrong; let's camp by plane, and, by the way, my old Scout Master used to say "any fool can be uncomfortable;" and the Hudson's Bay Company says, "there is little object in traveling tough just for the sake of being tough."

GEAR

Countless camping books have checklists of camping equipment (including the author's own *Lightplane Vacationing*—Editor's note) and there is no need to go into all the basics here.

SHELTER

Because you are not carrying it, it need not be the lightest since the price dif-

Don't hesitate to take any problem or camping question to the professionals. Here, the famous L. L. Bean store in Maine is a mecca for the outdoor pilot.
Photo Credit: E. G. Anderson

ference of a few pounds or ounces can be incredible. Because of the hoped-for proximity of your aircraft to the campsite, you do not need the best backpack, nor for occasional use, the best tent. Any Sears Roebuck type rip stop nylon pup tent with a plastic fly sheet is good enough. Rubber or foam mattresses are light but bulky, and air mattresses which are heavier but take up less room, may be more practical, unless you really need good insulation. At least one air mattress is a good idea in case you are in a survival situation with rivers or swamps. Almost any type of sleeping bag is adequate for occasional use. We have goose down, and ones with Dupont Fiberfill II but tend to end up using our softer, less noisy, cheap Coleman bags which I think cost only about $10.00. Ponchos or sheets of plastic complete the requirements for shelter.

TARPAULIN TENTS

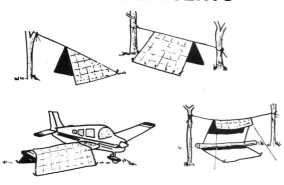

A good night's sleep is important and Harvey Manning points out that the setting of the sun can be a "poignantly sad event" reminding the camper of the night's misery ahead.

CLOTHING

Clothing need not be covered here in detail other than to say that weather changes should be anticipated and enough clothes carried for a complete change. I once got flooded out of a tent in Minnesota in a dreadful storm and had to hike a couple of miles along a lake in the dark to make a radio telephone call. I was stark nude under my poncho since I had

no dry clothes, and when I rang a woman's doorbell to make the radio call, she said, "Come in and take off your poncho!" Come to think of it, she was a pretty good looking girl, too—for 72. Some woolen clothing is ideal as it still insulates even if wet. Long sleeve shirts and full length pants may be helpful against insects, poison ivy, sunburn and thorns. String vests can be useful since they insulate both against cold and heat. Break in your footwear before the trip and carry plenty of spare socks, a hat and maybe a pair of cheap cotton work gloves. A bandana is always useful as a hat or sling. Sunglasses, you already have in the plane, but carry a spare.

Shelter — clothing — what's next?

COOKWARE

How much you carry depends on your plans. It is hard to get too enthused about cooking if you are landing at airstrips with eating facilities. Somehow, I seem to grudge buying a bed for the night, but not a meal. Maybe that is because I am awake for one service but not the other. Maybe the answer is to stay awake all night in order to feel you are getting the value of your hotel bed! Good quality cookware is worth the difference in price—thin aluminum spreads heat unevenly and the pans don't last. Your choice of pans will depend on your choice of stove as many are arranged to fit or complement each other. The Sigg Tourist Set and the Smilie both pack neatly, designed for the Svea 123 Stove which seems to be everyone's favorite. The Svea 123 weighs only 18 ounces and takes one third of a pint (four ounces) of white unleaded gas. The older one-half pint Primus 71 (Optimus 80) weighs 20 ounces but lacks a self-cleaning needle. The self-cleaning Optimus 111-B weighs 3½ pounds but has a useful manual pump for use at altitude.

Kerosene stoves are dirty and smelly but fuel is readily available, even in remote areas. They are safe and cheap.

Butane is popular but heavy, expen-

Beach camping and lake camping remind many pilots that their passengers came more for the end result than the journey itself. Photos Credits: Cessna Aircraft Company and Beech Aircraft Corporation

sive, slow, smelly if it leaks and freezes easily and does poorly at altitude.

Propane beats butane on those scores. It is, however, heavy, but my favorite for plane camping is the Primus 2361 Grasshopper which weighs only 12 ounces but a 6-hour propane cylinder weighs two pounds. The Grasshopper will take standard cylinders like Sears, Turner, Bernzomatic, etc.

Alcohol stoves, although non-toxic and non-explosive, are slow and really passe. Sterno solid fuel stoves, though cheap, are for back-up only as they are so slow.

It may not be very woodsy or glamorous to use a stove but it is more considerate of the forest, and the convenience of eating while others are still gathering firewood justifies it. The Grasshopper propane cylinder can be removed at any time and used on a lantern, too.

After shelter, clothing and cookware comes

FOOD

Those are the necessities of survival situations also and competence in camping gives resilience in survival. Food should be chosen for its lightness, compactness and ability not to waste or spoil under varied camping conditions, and maybe also ("Gosh dad! This is an endurance test!") for its taste. Prices in camping supply houses are almost impertinent and shopping in a good supermarket or ethnic delicatessen may be about as useful. Some ethnic bakery products like pumpernickel or dark whole grain bread may last for as long as two weeks. The sausage meats also keep very well, such as dauernwurst or salami, and bacon non sliced in slabs will last a long time. (If mold grows, it may still be eaten but cut off the mold if it bothers you.) Wilson's bacon bar is about one-third protein and one-third fat, the rest water; and is a useful form of pemmican: 3 ounces of it is equivalent to 12 ounces of raw bacon. Similar to it is Mountain House freeze dried sausage patties. Bouillon cubes are also tasty. Ground meat spoils the fastest. If you can handle the weight of canned goods, verify that they need no refrigeration. Other protein sources are peanut butter, cheese, eggs

Be honest—you don't see expressions like this in the back seat of the plane. Children need their days to be broken up. You are on a vacation, not an endurance test.
                                        Photo Credit: Margaret Anderson

39

Photo Credit: Charles L. Cashin, Jr.

Use your passengers to help stow baggage and try to load with the same routine each trip to prevent errors.

Piper Aircraft Corporation

and milk—both of which latter available in dried form, recall World War II but are still very useful. Oriental food shops often have lightweight dried foods cheaper than camping stores. For survival situations, you may want to investigate General Mills MPF—Modern Protein Food—designed for developing countries. It is a 4½ pound sealed can of defatted soy bean precooked 75 calories per ounce which can be eaten hot or cold, wet or dry.

There are also, from Europe, Maggi and Knorr soups. Dried legumes are popular. Drinks may be cocoa, coffee, tea, Ovaltine, bouillon, Lipton's soups and instant breakfast drinks.

Colin Fletcher recommends that for desserts you have instant puddings, instant fruit soups like the Swedish Ekstrom's or the Norwegian Bergene's, dried fruit, nuts, M&M chocolate, Hershey chocolate, hard candy, Lifesavers, Marzipan, raisins, Mountain House freeze dried ice cream and packets of granulated sugar. Carry a few salt tablets.

In theory, you need about 2 to 2½ pounds of freeze dried vacuum dried food per day, and they are excellent provided you have access to plenty of water. Don't believe the label, as they don't seem to satisfy as much in quantity as they are supposed to. The foil of those foods in a survival kit is handy for makeshift pans or signaling.

What do your troops think as you work away with those menus? Like Colin Fletcher, I am originally British and familiar with the statement "Hell has been described as a place where the politicians are French, the policemen German and the cooks British!" Mark you, I am a poor one to be giving cooking advice. After 14 years of marriage, my wife went to visit her mother and claims she had to show me how to work the coffee percolator before she left.

Colin Fletcher, the king of backpackers, saws off his toothbrush handle to travel light and even cuts the labels off his teabags!

Perhaps this is as good a place as any to mention natural foods. Ralph Johnson appeals to a Scot like me. "Live off the land. It is fun. And it doesn't cost a cent." I don't know about fun: in the early Colonial days in Jamestown, the settlers died after crop failures, and during the Civil War the Southerners had to relearn how to live off the land.

PLANT FOOD: There are about 300,000 known species of plants, of which 120,000 are edible and only a few poisonous. There are a few general rules. Plants and berries eaten by animals and birds are probably safe. Avoid plants with a milky sap or colored sap from cut branches. Avoid, probably, white or red berries or fruit (although tomatoes, strawberries and apples are safe, and red is a safer color in cold climates). Bitter taste is a warning—be careful with nuts and seeds. Test your senses in rotation: if a food looks good, if it smells good and if it tastes good, maybe it is safe. Since some poisons are water soluble, boil a bit of the food for one quarter of an hour, reject the water and hold a piece of the food in your mouth for five minutes. If it then seems okay, swallow it and wait eight hours; if you are still okay, eat more, wait another eight hours and then if you feel fine, the plant is okay. If in doubt, drop the plant into boiling water and change the water three times. Avoid all fungi. I don't care how smart you think you are at differentiating toadstools from mushrooms, I can still see that family in our Emergency Room in New Hampshire as they vomited their way into the ambulance for the trip to Boston that was going to save some of their lives. All from eating fungi. Even Euell Gibbons boiled his acorns for two hours and changed the water every time it became tea-colored (the water added was fresh and boiling each time).

If the food is safe, boiling conserves the value of food if you drink the water too; but some vitamins, especially Vitamin C, are destroyed by heat.

ANIMAL FOOD: Again, there are some general rules. All flesh is edible — exceptions: toads, some poisonous fish, the livers of polar bears and seals, and the Hawksbill Turtle (whatever that is). Parasites and their eggs are killed by heat and cooking. Fresh meat is free from bacterial infection, and can be preserved by smoking, sun drying, pickling, salting, cooking and freezing. Three ounces of fresh meat loses about two ounces of weight due to water loss.

Spoiled meat is a problem. Should you find it in survival situations, you probably should not eat it even if you cook it. The animal may have died due to illness or now be contaminated. There are some poisons which are not inactivated by heat. The germ Clostridium botulism can form on decayed meat and is one of the most potent poisons known to man. I once knew an M.D. who saw some being prepared in Europe to satisfy a Corsican vendetta. The meat was hanging as a rotten carcass and toxin was dropping off like melting ice into a collecting system of bottles. The peasant told the doctor that there was enough in the bottles to kill the entire village.

Lower forms of life are easier to catch than higher and if it moves, you can eat it. In this category you have amongst insects: ants, grubs, larvae, grasshoppers; amongst the reptiles: frogs, lizards, snakes and turtles; and also game birds.

FISH: Reject any fish which is ugly or of unusual shape or lacks scales (see chapter on Overwater Flying). Some tropical fish go bad within a few minutes of death if uncooked. Captain Cook's men "fell a-vomiting violently ill with the poison of the fish they had eaten." Fresh water shellfish should always be cooked in case of sewage or parasitic contamination.

For how to trap and snare animals, the reader is referred to the excellent book by the Australian author Richard Graves *Bushcraft* (c) 1972 Dymock's Book Arcade. The Swedish book *Wilderness Survival* by pilot Berndt Berglund (c) 1972 Pagurian Press Ltd, also covers this subject well.

Here are some general points on snaring animals: Look for game trails around your camp but keep referring back to your landmarks to avoid getting lost. You can experiment with your snares using different baits to see what animals are around and what they are likely to go for. When you set snares, remember they are working for you 24 hours a day and they should be visited often to prevent excessive animal suffering.

Use snares for small animals, don't waste ammunition on them. Birds can be caught with bait on fishing hooks.

To remove the human smell from snares, they can be scorched with fire once they are set up, or they can be made with hands scented with aromatic plants crushed in the fingers as the trap is made.

A lure should be added in the form of food or bait.

You have to overcome your aversion to eating fresh foods or dressing meats if you are to survive in the wilderness.

It is not recommended that on a routine camping trip you ignore your ground meat in the plane and eat berries; but in a true survival situation, you must find food. People have died of starvation surrounded by plenty—because they were ignorant. Part of the trouble is that we are so well nourished from our sophisticated gluttony that we tolerate badly the slightest deprivation. Walter Winchell used to say that most people ate as if their stomachs belonged to someone else.

Before we get back to plane camping, let's just revise methods of purifying *water*. Water may be boiled to purify. Halazone tablets can be used where one tablet is added to one pint of water. The water is then agitated to remove the odor but hold your nose when you drink it.

Iodine from your First Aid Kit can be used in a dose of two to four drops of iodine per quart of water. Bleach, in a similar dose, can be used. For example, Clorox, Purex, etc. Use the upper dose only if the water is very turbid. It is said that a rushing, bubbling stream cleans itself over sand and stones in 30 feet.

OTHER ITEMS OF CAMP GEAR TO CONSIDER:

KNIVES are ancient tools going right back to the Stone Age and probably, along with a means of starting a fire, are the most important of all the survival needs. There are all types and costs of sheath knives, though folding knives are more alike. A 3-4½ inch blade is ideal. Remember not to store a sheath knife in the leather sheath as the extracts oil from the knife and rusts it.

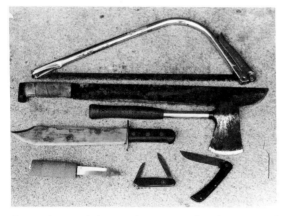

A cutting tool is a prime necessity for survival. Clockwise bottom right: Case "sod buster," Swiss army knife, floating survival knife, Bowie knife (ideal), small ax, machette (useful in the desert), small saw. YOU MUST HAVE AT LEAST ONE.
Photo Credit: E. G. Anderson

A SMALL AX is useful and Richard Frisbie says the camper is not a man until he's shaved with an ax. A small shovel or trowel may also be required. The U.S. Army ⅛-ounce can opener will also double as a screwdriver

What else is required in the kitchen line—aluminum foil, some baggies, some Gerry polytubes, a nylon stuff bag to hang food in at least 12 feet above the ground in bear country

(never, never keep food in your tent there).

FLASHLIGHT: Several inexpensive ones are more useful than a family heirloom that you might leave somewhere. The Mallory Duracell 805 is only 2½ ounces with batteries; the alkaline batteries last three times longer. Don't put batteries in till needed and carry spare bulbs.

BINOCULARS add a new dimension to a camping trip and may be useful in the air if you are lost! 7x35 are the best all-round size = 7 times the magnification and 35 the diameter in millimeters for gathering light. 7x50 is excellent for night work. 9x35 needs a tripod and is too bulky and has too much tremor for aircraft use. The old idea was that the diameter should be five times the magnification figure but now excellent 7x20 and 8x21 sets are on the market.

What else: toilet kit with the smallest tube of toothpaste, suntan lotion, lip balm, insect repellent, soap, washcloth, brush, comb, deodorant, some first aid extras like foot powder, alcohol, mirror, razor, scissors, toilet roll and sunglasses.

A repair kit with some rip stop tape, needle, thread, nylon cord, spare boot laces, sharpening stone, dental floss, rubber bands, plastic bags and empty 35 mm film cans which are excellent for odds and ends.

Since we are having to trudge through the monotony of checklists, let's just jot down the survival list of the Sierra Club for its ten essentials.

1) Complete change of clothing; cold and wet weather; 2-ounce space blanket
2) Food
3) Fire starters
4) Emergency matches
5) Flashlight
6) Knife
7) Sunglasses
8) First Aid Kit
9) Maps and compass
10) Whistle

FIRE STARTING
Many methods and they all work. Clockwise bottom right: Battery steel wool, lens, small candle and book of matches which fit into 35mm film can, various waterproof matches, "iron match," fire ribbon, commercial tinder.
Photo Credit: E. G. Anderson

A gun, also, might be a necessary or a desirable item in your survival kit. One authority recommends the over-and-under Savage Model 24V which has 30-30 and twenty gauge 3-inch magnum barrels. This is a simple, rugged, short, light, folding, inexpensive weapon. Don't forget ammunition.

Water canteens should also be carried.

SKILLS

FIRE STARTING

Remember the old country saying, "the bigger the fire, the bigger the fool," and the Indian adage: "White man build big fire, stand far away. Indian build small fire, stand close."

80% of all forest fires are caused by campers. A treetop fire can travel at 200 miles an hour, destroying the wilderness. If you want it to be around for your future children, don't cause a forest fire.

Starting a fire is easier if you have

RUB AGAINST TOP OF BATTERY

steel wool 00 or finer

SQUEEZE TIGHT

FIRE STARTING

prepared yourself for this with your supplies.

1) The easiest method is by using matches, which should be kept waterproof by nail polish, lacquer, candle grease or any other waterproof material. Matches, used with a candle, are probably the easiest way of starting a fire and a small 35mm film can will hold a kit nicely. Slip in a piece of sandpaper with the kit and use sealing wax on the metal thread of the can.

2) Artificial tinder can be bought for kindling.

3) Batteries and steel wool will work if you are patient.

4) Magnifying glass or lens can be used and requires even more patience.

5) Flint and steel, commercial or natural, can be used. Occasionally striking rocks containing iron pyrites or "fool's gold" will give you a spark. A cigarette lighter is useful even when it is out of fuel because of the contained flint.

6) Gunfire; remove the shot, pour half of the powder onto the tinder. Place a rag in the cartridge and fire into the air.

7) The Indian bow and drill method really does work but it is much more hard work and complicated than at first sight. A description is contained in any camping book but a lot of elbow grease is required and Richard Frisbie points out that Indians using this method were seldom fat.

Using natural tinder in dry weather requires you to collect minute twigs and hold as a bundle like an old fashioned broom. Tease some bark fiber or dried grass or dried leaves or pine needles into the center, then ignite the mass like a torch and use it to light your fire. Cup your hand with the match as wind protection and use your body as a wind break.

In wet weather, cut into some wet sticks until you have reached the dry center, then raise fuzz or layers of stick—heck, do I really have to go into such details? Weren't you in the Scouts too? If it is really wet, you may have to light a small fire

in one of your billy cans.

There is a knack to starting a new fire from a hot coal. Make a ball of tinder like dried grass or teased bark fiber, place the coal spark in the center, then whirl the ball in your loose hand above your head. Then blow vigorously between your fingers, which will make the tinder start to smoke, then flame. A couple of plastic straws are useful in your cooking gear. They can be used to blow the fire like a bellows to help a fire get started and can also be used to collect water from rock fissures or other seepage areas, and as part of your solar still (see Desert Flying).

Always gather as much firewood as you think you will need, then double it. Carry enough matches and conserve them. If you are wet, don't lean over your tinder and don't light your fire under snow branches. Guard against flying embers as boots and equipment will easily burn. Fire is the most important factor in wilderness survival and only a fool would venture into remote areas without a method of starting fire. If you have no fuel to burn, you can mix dirt, oil and gasoline in cans and burn them.

COOKING WITH MINIMAL GEAR

Boiling water without pans can be done relatively easily. Dig a hole and line with a poncho, a cloth or even a shirt. Fill with water and heat a couple of dozen small stones each the size of a baby's fist. When the stones are nearly red hot, they can be dropped into the water to make it boil. The cloth won't burn.

COAT HANGER INTO FRYING PAN

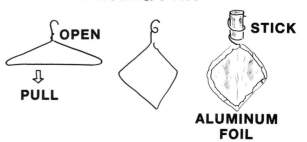

OPEN

PULL

STICK

ALUMINUM FOIL

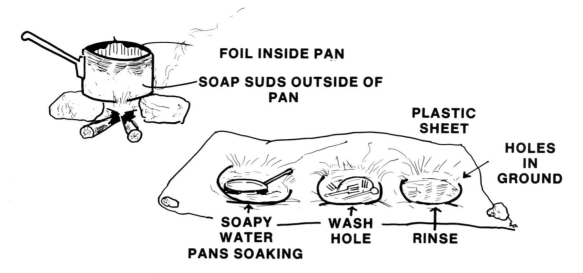

FOIL INSIDE PAN

SOAP SUDS OUTSIDE OF PAN

PLASTIC SHEET

HOLES IN GROUND

SOAPY WATER PANS SOAKING

WASH HOLE

RINSE

DISH WASHING EASE WITHOUT THE PROPER GEAR

Instead of cooking utensils, a flat stone may be heated until very hot, then dusted off. Meat can be laid on it to cook, which will be a satisfactory method for bacon, eggs and any flat or easily cooked dish. Do not use stones from riverbeds as they may explode when hot. Holes can be dug in the hot ground under the fire and food buried in wet clothes, clay or paper. The fire is then reconstructed again over the "oven." Eggs can be boiled in paper cups or simply placed in hot ashes to roast, but first the shell and inner membrane has to be pierced to allow steam and water vapor to escape.

HOMEMADE LAMPS

COAT HANGER CUT THEN FASTENED

CAN BOTH ENDS CUT OUT

NAIL

CANDLE LANTERN

HOMEMADE CANDLE HOLDER

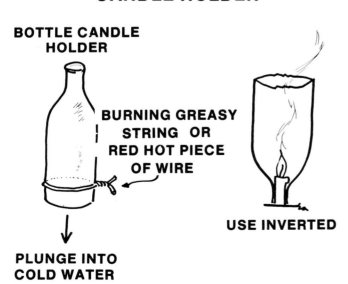

BOTTLE CANDLE HOLDER

BURNING GREASY STRING OR RED HOT PIECE OF WIRE

USE INVERTED

PLUNGE INTO COLD WATER

TWIG

RAG

FAT FROM COOKING

DIRT

OLD CAN

SLUSH LAMP

Camping may be a simple picnic by a riverside (Photo Credit: Cessna Aircraft Company) or a survival experience in the mountains of Colorado — so — BE PREPARED. BE EQUIPPED.

Photo Credit: Colorado Travel Section

Before you land, circle your remote strip to locate any potential campsite.
Photo Credit: Vermont Agency of Development and Community Affairs

LAYING OUT THE CAMP

Study the layout of the land, paying attention to wind direction, drainage and sun direction and exposure. Avoid low lying ground or you will be more miserable than you need be. (My wife, not exactly the complete camper, disputes that it is ever possible in any way for camping to be any more miserable than it normally is.) Avoid game trails and heavy trees, for obvious reasons. In mosquito season, stay away from wet areas and look for a gentle breeze to keep bugs away.

PLANNING THE VACATION

Some general points emerge:
1) Get familiar with the plane before the journey starts.
2) Stow away possessions and gear in the plane in an orderly constant fashion.
   Don't overload, but travel light. Wear wash-and-wear.
3) Try to avoid the busy weekend flyer by starting and ending your trips midweek.
4) Don't make each day too long. Stop to stretch your legs and unstretch your bladder every two to three hours. Eat light meals while traveling and try to finish each leg by mid afternoon.
5) Avoid get-homeitis. Don't litterbug. Conserve the wilderness.
6) Remember Robert Wood. "Nothing dooms a trip like slipshod preparation. It only takes one or two mistakes." I think Wood was being generous—in flying, it only takes one.

For further reading, the reader is referred to Colin Fletcher, a dreamer and a poet with a pack, *The Complete Walker* (c) Alfred A. Knopf, Inc., New York.

4
ENDURANCE
AND
SURVIVAL

"If a person can endure this voyage within
his own experience, he can emerge from it
with a new concept."

Sidney Jourard

ENDURANCE AND SURVIVAL

Introduction

Your Enemies in the Wilderness —
    Psychological Aspects of Survival

After the Crash
    First Priorities
    Survival Kits
    Signaling
    Walking Out

Pilots are more familiar with the "numbers" for their aircraft than they are with the statistics for their own body. Their plane is probably in better shape, too.

At all times, have your emergency landing site picked out and part of your scan should assess surface winds.

Photo Credit: Beech Aircraft Corporation

Whether you are stranded in a desolate area as a result of an aircraft forced landing or through choice because you are camping the wilderness, you may be interested in knowing that your body is capable of unbelievable feats.

In 1792, a man age 77 ran the 200 miles between Liverpool and London in four days. A decade later in 1808, a man ran 1,000 miles in 1,000 consecutive hours for 1,000 guineas (that's 21 shillings, worth about $4.50 then.). In 1823, one Hugh Glass was mauled by a bear and left to die by his friends. Despite many broken bones, he crawled 100 miles in several

months to reach the Cheyenne River. He then floated 150 miles downstream on a log to reach Fort Kiowa.

More recently, we see that in February 1928, an American Indian, Andy Payne, won a prize of $25,000 in a 3422 mile foot race across the United States. He averaged six miles per hour for 525 hours! You know, a man ran 160 miles in 24 hours in England; the impressive thing to me being that he was 45 years old, my age.

In 1950, a Mau Mau African called Dedan was pursued over very rough country by varying police groups who took turns to rest. He ran 350 miles in three and a half days.

Actually, medically, your ability to conquer a threatening survival situation depends on several factors. Your body build is important. Fat persons, like camels, have more food in reserve and can endure cold more due to the increased insulation. Their relatively low surface area per pound is a problem when they wish to lose heat however.

Training will improve endurance capabilities but some people are better than others even in an untrained state. Why? Apparently it is a combination of luck and genetic endowment. Some people are born with relatively slow heart rates, making them magnificent machines capable of great efforts from such low cardiac baselines. The renowned distance runners Gunder Hagg and Paavo Nurmi had resting pulse rates of 35, so if you are lost in the Arctic and have to team up with a luscious blonde or a gorgeous redhead, choose the redhead if she has got a slow pulse rate.

So don't underestimate your own body if it faces its greatest challenge. Never give up. In fact, determination and spiritual confidence are as important as physical strength. And what strength we see elsewhere in Nature. Sooty Terns are said to fly *non-stop* for three to five years after leaving their birthplace. Lesser Yellowlegs fly 1,900 miles from New England to the West Indies in six days, and Golden Plovers fly 2,400 miles non-stop from East Canada to South America in their migrations. Even the Pacific salmon is impressive; 500 to 1,000 miles upstream (How's that for head winds?) non-stop in twelve days.

Don't fret if you haven't yet had a chance to prove your worth. It's around the corner! The American Disaster Research Group feels you have one chance in a lifetime of being a helper or a victim of a natural disaster. Ten million coastal Americans are constantly endangered by floods, with lack of training causing many drownings. There are thousands of deaths in Europe when the northern coastline of that continent from Holland to Germany gets flooded. Some die there because they lack the primary skills for initial survival, some because of mob curiosity reactions which block rescue attempts, and some because of lack of rehearsal of the ambulance and medical personnel.

Man often has to be rescued from his stupidity or ignorance. For example, 2,000 are annually brought down from the Austrian Alps. Two thousand! But there are other ways to be careless . . . in the United States, 1,000 die smoking in bed and 150 a year poison themselves accidentally. Let's be more cheerful.

There are others who have proved the value of training, enthusiasm and confidence.

In 1956, nine Frenchmen survived a trial existence with only bows and arrows, earthenware pots and sheepskins. In 1960, fourteen Europeans climbed into the French Alps dressed in ordinary clothes and lived in snow huts at 9,000 feet built with bare hands. Two days later, they had an experimental air drop of food and equipment, and came down . . . all alive . . . six days later. However, the same year saw a French group nearly die in an experiment in the Sahara.

In 1962 the Australian, Bill Penman, lived for two months in a cave; a record surpassed the same year when 23-year-old Michael Siffre spent 62 days 300 feet below the earth's surface.

However, pilot interest in survival goes further back than that. In 1949, Curtis E. Lemay realized that pilots were being taught to fly but not to survive. He arranged for Strategic Air Command pilots to be trained at Carson Air Force Base in Colorado, then at Stead in Nevada "120 degrees in the shade in summer and so cold in winter that your tongue might freeze." The pilots were taught to "eat anything that doesn't eat you." I have a friend who had Green Beret training in Panama who did their survival course. They would grab any non poisonous snake, wrap it around their waists alive to keep it fresh under their shirts until they were hungry. The military are always interested in survival incidents and interview the survivors of any event to study deaths and to learn from life.

What can you learn from those rescued? Certainly, what your enemies are.

Your Enemies in the Wilderness Psychological Aspects of Survival

It has been said that the five basic human requirements in survival are water, food, heat, shelter and spiritual needs. Subtract any two from that list of five and the results are likely to be fatal.

(1) FEAR AND PANIC: This sensation is felt by all who are stranded in the wilderness. It has to be fought in a positive manner. It is no big deal to be lost and stranded in a remote area . . . it has happened to many persons. Force yourself to sit down and think. Talk to yourself. Remember the old R.O.T.C. advice for any situation: Object. Factors. Courses. Plan.

Object: To get out alive.

Factors: You have a survival kit, including a sectional map and a compass. You have training and know how to find water. You are near an air route. You filed a flight plan.

Courses: Stay put forever till found. Stay put for one week, then walk out. Walk out now.

Plan: Stay put one week, then reconsider.

By sitting down and using reason, by being cerebral and not a headless animal, fear quietens down and does not lead to panic. I remember once being in a National Guard Parachute Regiment which returned from Germany after military exercises. The Flying Boxcar (C 119) over the British airport did not get a green on lowering the undercarriage and the Adjutant on the ground had to make a decision about his civilian soldiers above him. He ordered the Paratroopers to bail out and then watched his men breaking limbs on the concrete in a stiff wind (we never routinely jumped in ground winds above 18 knots). The man in charge, being a regular professional officer, probably saw his career folding in the to-be-expected Court of Inquiry and gave orders sending the same man in different directions but simultaneously. Fear builds up to panic; it's easy for me to be critical as it wasn't my career that was on the line.

(2) PAIN AND FATIGUE creep up slowly to make a person less efficient. Pain may be obvious from the beginning if there is an injury during the crash. It is emphasized by the isolation of your situation. At night when you are not distracted by your busy day, pain will be more obvious. Know, therefore, that you will be more likely to suffer during the quiet of the night. Know, understand and accept this and don't be demoralized by the phenomenon.

I have a doctor friend who, in a rural area of Texas, is run off his feet night and day by a demanding solo practice. He has a sign above his desk, "A pain at 3 a.m. is no worse than a pain at 3 p.m.!"

Fatigue can make you escape into a dull-witted, non reality such as falling asleep in the snow. Avoid it by organizing your day and not overdoing things. Remember the old adage: Never stand when you can sit, never sit when you can be lying down.

(3) COLD numbs the will to endure, which is why a means of lighting a fire is so important. Cold kills. In November 1682, there was a ship wreck near Boston Harbor during a snowstorm. The crew got ashore to a sandy beach two hours later but many died in the snowdrifts inland. Cold kills.

(4) HUNGER AND THIRST can dominate your survival thoughts. Hunger is a primitive feeling; we assuage it so promptly in our affluent life that we are ill-prepared to meet it in the wilds. Hunger can be endured as Ghandi showed with his political fasts. An Indian fakir once fasted for 81 days and a German for 79 days with a loss of 87 pounds.

A member of Shackleton's expedition is quoted, "We all seem to live for food and think of nothing but food," and Richard Howard, a survivor of a lost Arctic party, stated that hunger was so painful that they agreed not to discuss food "but by the next day by tacit consent, they had all come back to the same subject." The Andes survivors constantly thought of food and had competitions to see who could describe the best menu, games which stopped when they feared their dreams would stimulate ulcers. The three airmen, Dixon, Pastula and Aldrich, floating for 34 days in the open Pacific in World War Two had fantasies that they would eat and gorge for three days at each other's houses when rescued.

The tales of shipwreck and sea survival are tales of hunger and thirst, but people have succumbed in land

53

situations surrounded by plenty. Unbelievably, persons have died of thirst with ample water nearby simply because they forgot to drink. A good discipline is to make yourself drink a quart of water every night as you turn in. If you are dehydrated, you won't have much urinary output and dark, scanty, concentrated urine is a signal to drink more. You should be passing two to three pints of urine a day (see Desert Flying).

Don't eat any of your survival food on your first day as you probably ate well the day before, to give you a reservoir.

(5) LONELINESS AND BOREDOM are your last enemies in survival. They are even "unexpected visitors" to a nighttime campfire when camping. Not everyone can tolerate solitude as was found out in astronaut selection. The only child is more able to handle loneliness, and those from large families accept it badly. Survival expert Anthony Greenbank points out the value of prayer and that your bad situation can be accepted as never likely to get worse. He reminds us never to give in by saying, "never, never, never, never, never never, never give up trying." Outdoorsman Bernt Berglund points out, "it is better to do something rather than nothing, even if it is the wrong thing."

Talk to yourself, make notes, keep a diary which you can re-read, and sing. My music teacher at school used to weed out the people with flat voices by encouraging them during singing to sing loudly. The bad singers were soon traced and stuck at the back of the class. Actually, it wasn't too bad at the back of the class. I quite enjoyed it. However, this music teacher used to say, "when in doubt, shout," and that is not bad advice for the wilderness. Improvise games. In a group situation, pool your resources and learn the skills of group members. Select a leader and if a

choice is difficult, why not go for the guy who was so smart he bought this book! But even in a group, expect boredom. In 1961 a newspaper reporter, Harvey Boyd, tried an experiment. With his family, he attempted to endure a survival situation near San Francisco to simulate the aftermath of a nuclear war and failed after twelve days.

Physical demands can overwhelm you, but refuse to let them. Be greater than you could hope to be. Remember one of the most dramatic events in athletics: "My body had long since exhausted its energy, but it went on running just the same. The physical overdraft came only from greater willpower." *Four Minute Mile*, Roger Bannister (c) 1955, Dodd Mead & Co.

Finally, remember the word "survive" comes from the Latin super . . . above, beyond . . . and vivo . . . I live. Practice it. Your brain is your best survival weapon. Use it. Think. Improvise. In talking to relatives in medical catastrophies, doctors ask them to expect the worst but hope for the best; this is sound advice, too, to give yourself in any lonely survival situation.

Let us imagine that you have just successfuly landed or crashed your plane in a remote area. Let us consider the generalities involved.

After the Crash

The plane was prepared for the forced landing as best you could. The fuel was turned off, the ignition, too; and once the desired degree of flaps achieved, the master also. You have flown the aircraft to the end at its slowest speed and tried to fly it forward into the ground rather than stalling and falling with vertical deceleration. The body can stand horizontal compression strain more than vertical.

Hold on tight until the plane stops moving, then try to get up fast as there is danger of fire. Throw out your survival kit quickly for the same reason. In a statistical survey of a large number of general aviation accidents, 6% burned on impact and 60% of the fires had fatal outcomes. In Vietnam, the U.S. Army noted to its anguish that many of its pilots, through skill, avoided injury in the forced landing, only to perish in the resultant fire.

If the plane does not immediately ignite, probably, probably, it is not going to. If you are trapped in the wreckage you should, therefore, try to relax since you can wriggle out better if you are not stiff and rigid. Look down and around; what is holding you in? Perhaps if you took off a belt with a large buckle or shrugged out of your boots, you could get out. Of course, Douglas Bader, trapped in his burning Spitfire, was lucky. He simply disconnected his artificial legs.

In trying to extricate a passenger, talk him out. Get him to relax. Don't yank him tight and compound a problem. If you are outside the aircraft, keep an eye on the direction of any fuel seepage. Is it getting close to the hot engine?

You are now out, and far enough from the plane to be safe from any fire. Check yourself and the others for injuries. There may be a delayed emotional reaction ranging from manic elation to agitated depression. Don't make significant decisions at this stage, and don't run around like a headless chicken overorganizing your situation. Any activity is best spent preparing shelter as long as you have daylight. Shelter should be basic . . . perhaps a hole dug beside a log and lined with spruce branches or soft brush. Don't make a fetish of braiding and plaiting branches in Boy Scout machismo; just throw together a basic shelter, then get cracking on firewood and fire. You need more wood than you think to last the night. No, that's still not enough. In fact, about ten armfuls is required. If there is no wood available, and you have a can of oil, empty it. Save the oil. Fill the can with dirt, pour in some gas and a touch of oil. Stand back and throw a burning branch at it. It may ignite with an explo-

A successful landing is one you survive and you're more likely to make it if it's a power-on precautionary landing while you're still VFR.

Photo by Hoover—Bureau of Aviation, Pennsylvania Department of Transportation

sion but then will burn more steadily. Even if matches are plentiful, don't let your fire go out. Never waste matches.

Check the contents of your survival kit. Look for items for warmth. Ration food and water.

Get out your signaling gear as the first plane you see may be the only one.

Now with shelter built and insulated, fire started and protected, you can turn back to the aircraft. Is the radio working? How is the battery? Did the ELT go off? If manually operated, should you spare its battery until the passage of time has alerted outside ears to listen, or should you set it off now? Most authorities think you should delay.

Look around, but don't leave the scene. Try to orient yourself. Where is the sun, where is the Pole star once night comes? Get out your sectional, which, hopefully, you didn't have to use for starting your fire. A hot drink before turning in works wonders, out of all proportion to its cost, but avoid a heavy meal at bedtime in cold weather. If your clothes are sodden with sweat, you will be warmer sleeping nude in a sleeping bag. Two in a bag is even warmer (come on now, be serious). If you have got dry socks, wear them because if your feet are warm and dry, your whole body feels warm.

Replenish the fire through the night and maintain a cheerful front to your passengers.

In the morning, you will be better able to orient yourself by reference to the direction of sunrise or by checking the area for Nature's clues. Moss really does grow on the shaded north side of rocks and trees, but choose several locations to get an average. On any tree stump, the bark is thicker on the cold north side and the orientation by sun is simplicity itself. Insert a stick about three feet tall vertically into the ground and put a stone at the top end of its shadow. Wait 15 minutes and repeat. A line continued from the first stone to the second points West. You can watch the shadows and when the stick shadow is at its shortest,

the shadow is pointing true North.

Things are now looking better. You know roughly where you are and can orientate your map. If your watch is broken and aircraft clock likewise, you can even tell solar time by constructing a sundial, but that discussion is beyond the scope of this book.

Again, you should check for injuries and assess your survival kit and rations. Your most pressing needs will depend on your locality. Don't lose anything from your supplies; if you must scatter things around, do it on a poncho or space blanket and don't let the wind or wild animals deplete your possessions. Pool any personal equipment; you are going to have to survive as a group.

Verify that your signals are displayed, then check the aircraft again. If your off-airport landing was less than a crash and you are close to traveled roads or air routes, then perhaps the plane will later be flown out and shouldn't be cannibalized. But if it is a complete wreck and stuck right in the middle of a forest, you have just lost an aircraft and may as well complete the tearing apart for materials. Look critically at the aircraft and ask what does it have that might be useful (see Walking Out section).

Panels of aluminum can be unscrewed or cut off, then wired together to make sleds, windbreaks, shelters and signals. The aluminum is not an insulator and without adding padding from the seat or natural materials, it will provide shelter too hot in the sun and too cold in inclement weather. This is why trapped, injured people boil in the desert inside metal planes and freeze inside them in winter.

For permission to reprint the following survival kit drawing and photograph from the author's book, *Lightplane Vacationing*, we are grateful to Crown Publishers, Modern Aircraft Series and TAB Books.

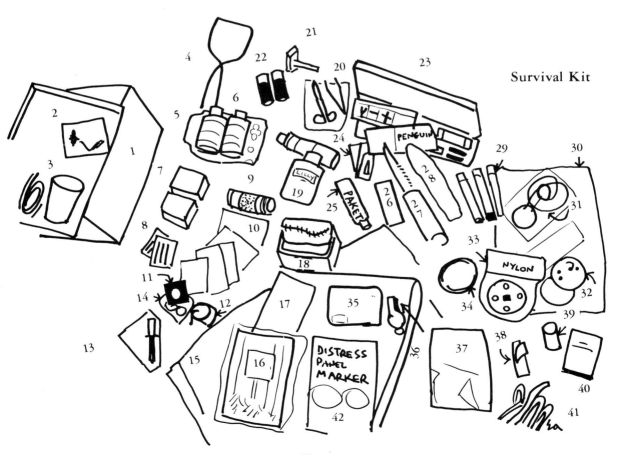

Survival Kit

SURVIVAL KIT

1. Box to hold 5 pound survival kit
2. Illustration of desert still
3. Plastic cup, plastic tubing to make desert still
4. Fishing net for catching bait for fishing
5. Bandanna neck tie for sling, hat, etc.
6. Cutter insect repellent
9. Waterproof matches
10. Packages of synthetic kindling to start fire
11. Cheap lens to start fire by sun
12. Candle to assist fire lighting
13. Metal match
14. Water purifying tablets
15. Burlap bag to hold box
17. Survival manuals
18. Compass
19. Lotion and tube of cream, Surfadil for sunburn (Lilly)
20. Disposable scissors and tweezers
21. Disposable shaver
22. Chap Stick
23. Flares and smoke grenades
24. Disposable scalpel blades
25. Tube disposable soap
26. Sharpening stone
27. Floating knife
28. Folding knife smeared with Vaseline and covered in plastic
29. Disposable flashlights
30. Aluminum foil for signaling, cooking pans, etc.
31. Folding saw
32. Fishing gear
33. Nylon line
34. Wire snares
35. Emergency space blanket sitting on larger space blanket
36. Whistle
37. Stainless steel signaling mirror
38. Can opener
39. Salt
40. Sewing kit
41. Nylon cord
42. Distress panel, orange marker

The electrical wires and control cables are a real source of building materials; fish lines, fish hooks and lures and God knows what a resourceful man could not do with a spanner and an engine. An antenna for the plane radio could be improvised, even light systems if the battery has some life.

Above all, keep up your spirits and know the human body is capable of great endurance. You don't need to burn up energy in the first few days looking for food. Your state of prenutrition will protect you initially. Don't ration water if there is plenty. As has been said, "ration sweat . . . not water." It is the water in your body that saves your life, not the water in your canteen.

The best survival kits are those you make up yourself. Just studying the contents of your magic box will remind you of survival ideas. Survival starts at home; solid thought and consideration of a future problem in survival in the convenience of your home before it happens, is going to pay dividends when the chips are down later in reality.

Signaling

The more different methods you use, the more likely you are to be spotted. Don't rely on any one method.

Try to make your area stand out from the rest of the land by clearing away snow or burning foliage. Spread out markers which may be logs or rocks or pieces of aircraft. Use sand or gravel to polish the paint off the surface of any aluminum material from the plane. Clear any dirt or snow from the surface of the plane.

If you are writing on the ground, use letters at least 25 feet long. Remember, it was only such huge ground signals that saved Ralph Flores and Helen Klaben after their plane crash. Always carry a card showing ground code letters in the glove compartment of your plane and in your survival kit.

Consider the other senses . . . make noises, remembering that three is the distress number whether it is three fires,

three ground crosses or three whistle blasts or gun shots. Do you remember that corny joke about the lost Indian who kept firing three arrows into the air but no one heard him?

If you have methods of lighting a fire, smoke is the cheapest of all signals, but look after your signal fires and protect them from the weather by having bark or spruce branches over them to keep them dry. Conserve any pyrotechnic devices and try to anticipate when you will use them. Think back to being a pilot and remember how blind you are below, when completely over a target. Signals, therefore, have to be sent to a plane that is not yet directly overhead.

More people have been rescued by the signaling mirror than by any other method. Practice with it. Get a friend to fly over your airstrip one day and practice until his wings are constantly waggling at your efficiency. Whether you have the mirror with the aiming hole or just a regular mirror, practice until you have got the system down to a fine art. Any piece of aluminum foil or metal can be used or even foil from foodstuffs. Just hold your left thumb extended, hit it with the light reflected from the mirror in your right hand, then bring your left thumb up to the aircraft, taking the beam with it. You can lay out panels of crinkled foil on rocks and some surfaces may be at just the right angle to flash at any aircraft overhead.

Walking Out

"Now bid me run, And I will strive with things impossible." Shakespeare.

You've finally made a decision. More than a week has gone by. You suspect the ELT has been faulty or not heard. You have recovered from the injuries of the crash and built up a stockpile of food and water. You surmise that any search has been called off or maybe you didn't even file a flight plan. You realize that it is up to you . . . you are going to have to save yourself. Can you? You bet! It will take guts and sweat, and maybe blood; but you are not going to quit. The decision for

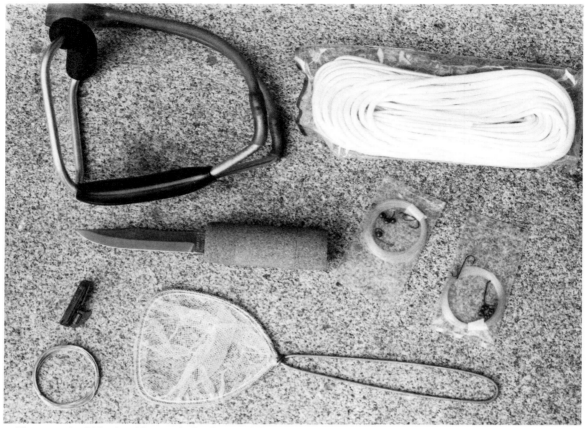

Your survival kit should contain basic material which enables you to live off the land. Clockwise, bottom right: bait net, snare wire, mini-can opener (my son, the photographer, has a sense of humor), sling shot, nylon cord, knife, fishing line and hooks. Photo Credit: Michael Anderson

action will probably rejuvenate you; it is soul destroying and tiring sitting tight and waiting.

First, again consider this decision to walk out. Is it the best idea? Are you in full view in an open desert close to Victor Airways with adequate water supplies? If so, maybe you should stay put. As you know, the literature is replete with stories of rescue parties finding empty planes and, later, dead walkers. Or, is your plane hidden forever in a deep forest or buried in a steep ravine that never sees daylight? If so, perhaps you will have to be more active and actually seek out salvation. Before you go, go over the plane wreckage again. What would be useful? Do you need the plane compass? Do you want the storage door or part of the wing as a sled? Can you use some lengths of wire? What about the seat covers to protect your footwear? Your shoes are actually going to take a beating. Remember Donn Fendler,

the 12-year-old boy who was lost for nine days on a mountain in Maine. His sneakers were slashed to bits within one day and Park Rangers tend to give new heavy sneakers a life of only about six trips even on regular tourist trails.

Go over the plane again, carefully searching in every pocket, below the seats and in the baggage area. You might find a map of the area, some string, a flashlight, even a knife. What about one of the lenses from cockpit lights as a future fire starter? Would the stripped off lining of the plane be of use as material? Could the sun visors be torn off to act as sandals or shovels? Could the seat belts and seat cushions be used to fabricate a back pack?

Could the metal of the seat springs be used for fish harpoons? Or ice crampons? Is the microphone flex of any use? Look at the outside. Could you cut up a tire to make rubber soled sandals? Could you use an inner tube for flotation? Can you use some of the screws or even the tail tie down ring? Could you turn part of the prop into a machette? Do you want the heavy battery, some wires and a light system? Do you want to carry some rubber and oil for fire signaling or even some gasoline for cautious fire starting?

small amounts often. Six pints a day is average for a normal trek and six quarts a day for steep terrain on a hot day. Water is a heavy load; a bush sled can be made from pieces of plane aluminum or from a six foot, Y-shaped branch with a load platform resting on the terminal Y. Backpackers do not carry more than 20%

IMPROVISED STRETCHER

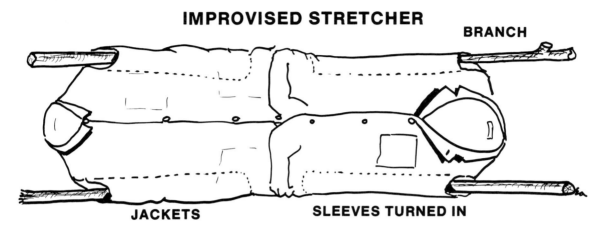

BRANCH

JACKETS　　　　**SLEEVES TURNED IN**

Okay. You're going! Put a note in the wreckage with the date, giving your intentions and direction of travel, and you're off. What is your plan? Do not overestimate your ability to cover distance; in fact, don't misjudge the distances themselves. In high, clear mountain air or clear desert atmosphere, multiply the distance you calculate by a factor of three. Are you fit enough for the work load? For interest, you burn up five calories per 100 pounds per hour just lying awake in bed. Walking two miles per hour burns 45 calories per 100 pounds per hour; three miles per hour doubles it to 90 calories and speeding up to four miles per hour costs 160 calories. In other words, go slow. Go steady. For example, running costs 320 calories per 100 pounds per hour.

A five foot staff should be cut from a convenient tree or made from aircraft wreckage. Try to pace yourself with a natural and comfortable rhythm. Don't make your rest stops too long as your muscles will stiffen. Each day, stop in time to make camp before it is dark and try to keep your fluid intake up by sipping

of their body weight and that is on properly designed back packs. That would mean a maximum load of about 35 pounds for your traditional 170 pound adult.

By now you are pretty hot and tired. You are glad you have worn a hat for shade, and in which you have cut ventilation holes. You are wearing a neckerchief around your neck for shade also. As you heat up, you are taking off your clothes in layers. To avoid chilling, you replace them as you rest. It probably is worth your while changing your socks every hour and hanging them around your neck to dry. Examine your feet for blisters and treat any as early as possible by band aid or, better, "moleskin" adhesive strips. Do not snip the blisters but leave alone unless they are wrinkled, when they should be cut away. Carry any talcum powder from your toilet kit and dust your feet every stop as you are depending on them more than you realize. As my Uncle Will used to say, travel broadens your feet! Jim Thorne, the American explorer, once borrowed boots in New Zealand for a trek without realizing there was a one size difference between the measurements of the

ON FINDING DIRECTION FROM NATURE

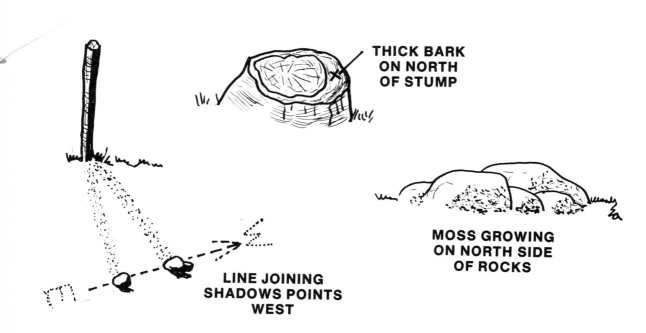

THICK BARK ON NORTH OF STUMP

MOSS GROWING ON NORTH SIDE OF ROCKS

LINE JOINING SHADOWS POINTS WEST

two countries. After a day of slipping and rubbing, he had five blisters on one foot and three on the other, with some the size of quarters. Therefore, wear enough socks to make your boots fit snugly. Long sleeve shirts and long pants are better for thorns, insects and sunburn. Jeans are pretty useless in wet terrain as they get stiff, wet and cold.

As you leave your camp each day, leave a note with intentions and direction of travel to help any ultimate search group. It is common in the Sierra Nevada, California, for three to four search and rescue groups to be going at any one time and since they do their bit willingly, it is almost criminal on your part not to try to help them. The problems of persons lost in the wilderness keep increasing and one National Park, for example, had 36 rescue missions in one season.

As you struggle on, walking out, don't develop tunnel vision and miss peripheral clues. Crash survivors have stumbled past recognizable trails and even signs of habitation but not noticed and kept on. Avoid the tendency, especially in forest and scrub, to walk in circles which some

think is due to the tendency of, say, a right-handed person always leaning to the right as he pushes aside brush while walking. The use of a compass and lining up three objects ahead in order to "hold a heading" is advised in close country. When you stop and rest, be sure to mark your direction of travel before you lie down.

Try to make a rough map as you go, in case you need to return. Attempt to judge your progress with reference to your total plan. Keep looking ahead to avoid a twisted ankle or a minor accident since you cannot afford to be injured, and also because you can respond early to obstacles by temporary change of direction. Bradford Angier has the slogan, "never step on anything you can step over, and never step over anything you can step around." Walk around lakes, don't try to swim across them.

If you have a definite destination in mind on your walk out, you may become confused as to whether you are to the left or right of it as you get closer. The method used by hunters in locating, say, a camp beside a river which is at right angles to

ON FINDING CAMP WHEN LOST

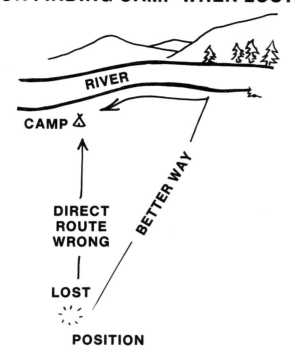

Holy Spirit. One gets his ideas by walking."

When you come into safety, do not overload your stomach immediately. When back in civilization, get back to a normal diet gently and gradually.

Don't forget to register your safe arrival with the relevant authorities. This will enable the FAA and local law agencies to tidy up their files to prevent future false rescue attempts should your trail or wreck be found by unknowing persons. This is a time, too, to give thanks to those concerned, including the Man upstairs.

their line of travel is to travel deliberately off by a few degrees to one side. Then, when the river is reached, the hunter knows which direction to turn in. I suspect some of us fly our cross countries this way, too!

Remember, you are not alone. Most survivors rescued from wilderness situations, even previous atheists, touch on the eerie feeling of being accompanied on their struggles as if they were being helped by an unseen force. Many felt unusual strength and resolve after prayer. You are not "a private ship on a private sea." Perhaps as you struggle along walking out you might be comforted by Nietzsche who has said, "The sedentary position is a positive hindrance to the

For further reading: *The Survival Book,* William K. Merrill, (c) 1972 Winchester Press.

Members of Coast Guard Training Team demonstrate basket hoist from surface vessel.
Photo Credit: U.S. Coast Guard

TOPOGRAPHICAL SYMBOLS

CITIES AND TOWNS

Metropolitan Areas _____ **NEW YORK**

Large Cities _____ **RICHMOND**

Cities _____ **ARLINGTON**

Small Cities _____ Freehold

Large Towns _____ Corville □

Towns & Villages _____ Arcola ○

HIGHWAYS AND ROADS

Dual Lane and Super Highways _____

Primary Roads _____

Secondary Roads _____

Trails _____

RELIEF FEATURES

Contours { Reliable _____
Approximate _____
Depression _____

Levees or Eskers _____

Hachures

Bluffs, Cliffs & Escarpments _____

Sand { Dunes _____
Areas _____
Ridges _____

Lava Flow _____

HYDROGRAPHIC FEATURES

Swamps & Marshes _____

Tidal Flats _____
(Exposed at low tide)

Rocks Awash _____

Shoals _____
(Exposed at low tide)

Springs _____

Wells & Water Holes _____

Reefs, Coral & Rocky Ledges _____
(Awash at low tide)

Streams & Rivers { Perennial _____
Intermittent _____
Probable or _____
Unsurveyed
Braided _____

Intermittent Lakes (blue stipple) _____

Drainage Ditches _____

Canals { In use _____
Abandoned _____

Dry Lake Beds (brown stipple) _____

Sand Deposits in river bed _____

Dry Washes (brown stipple) _____

Glaciers and Ice Caps _____

CULTURAL AND MISCELLANEOUS

Landmarks (with appropriate note) _____
(Numerals indicate elevation above sea level of top)
    ■ Factory
    ■ Stack 875'

Oil Tanks _____

Oil Fields _____

Dams _____

Elevations { Highest on chart _____ •1115
(In feet)   (Highest on chart is devoid of tint)
  Highest in a general area _____ •1085
  Spot _____ •950

Mines and Quarries _____

Mountain Passes _____)(

Lookout Stations (Elevation is base of tower) _____
  75 (Site)
  1025 (Elev)

Coast Guard Stations _____ ◆ CG 79

Pipe Lines _____ PIPE LINE

Race Tracks or Stadiums _____ RT

Stranded Wrecks _____

Boundaries { International _____
State & Provincial _____

Railroads { Abandoned or _____
Under Construction
Single Track _____
Multiple Track _____
Sidings & Spurs _____
Overpass _____
Underpass _____

Bridges { Railroad _____
Highway _____

Tunnels { Railroad _____
Highway _____

"*Intense sunlight, low humidity, hot dry winds, scanty rainfall; extreme fluctuations between day and nighttime temperatures. Survival under those conditions meant resolving two problems: how to handle excessive heat and how to avoid drying up.*"

Frank D. Venning

Quoted from CACTI, A Golden Guide
1974 Western Publishing Company, Inc.
Used by permission of the publisher.

5
DESERT FLYING

Photo Credit: Dana Downie

DESERT FLYING

Venning, a Naturalist, was actually describing cacti, but their problems parallel those of man and aircraft. There are many joys to desert flying: excellent visibility, spectacular scenery and dependable weather. But there is the inevitable other side of the coin which requires attention.

The desert requires understanding; it is a different milieu to what most of us are accustomed. It has been called a "harsh habitat" and throughout history, man has suffered its extremes. Most vacation fliers cross the desert during the summer season when the arid land below is at its most inhospitable and the lessons of desert flying are, therefore, essentially those of hot weather, density altitude and survival.

Let us consider those problems. Both pilot and plane have to be assessed when you've got the "hots" for flying the desert. How's your health? Have you any skin problems made worse by dry air and excessive solar radiation? Do you have dust respiratory allergies? Any eye problems?

Eat less in hot weather and drink plenty. Always take off to cross the desert with a stomach full of water (after all, you do have an empty coffee can behind you for relief). Wear sensible clothes comfortable for the desert by day yet adequate for the chill of evening. Carry a survival kit and supply of water adequate for the

In desert flying, have adequate water supply for each passenger and ensure that they all know where your survival kit is.
Photo Credit: Piper Aircraft Corporation

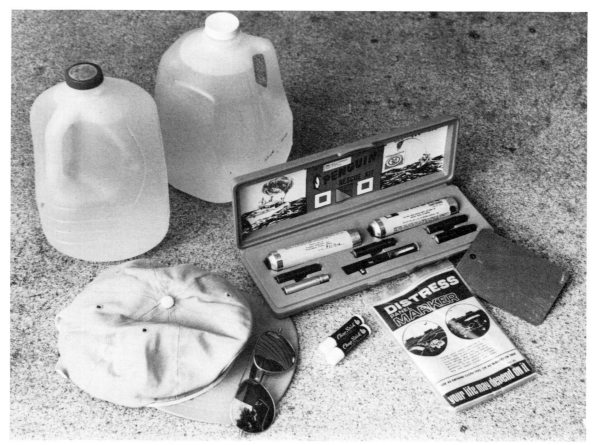

A minimum desert survival kit would include water supply, flares and smoke grenades, signaling mirror, ground marking panels, Chap Stick, sunglasses and headgear. Though water is heavy, the containers should be FULL.   Photo Credit: E. G. Anderson

personnel carried. Have a pair of light cotton gloves handy in case your control wheel becomes too hot to hold or in case you have to wrestle with a cactus. Know the maneuvering speed of your aircraft and get some practice in turbulent conditions. Heck, you know turbulence, you say. Have you ever sat in a seat with Charles Atlas striking with a 2x4 from below, Joe Frazier bouncing a rubber truncheon off your head and a first year dental student using a jackhammer on your teeth? Low hours pilots unaccustomed to the twisting hot air bubbles belching from hot desert floors have been known to panic and make errors in judgment as a result.

How's the plane? Do you have the heavier summer weight oil (and plenty of it as that helps keep your engine cool)? Do you have the right high enough octane rating for your fuel to avoid detonation?

Do you have 100 pound burlap bags, a small shovel and strong ropes for a tie-down kit? The manual should be familiar to you for data on techniques of hot starts.

Make sure you are not overloaded for the density altitude. Consider runway slope, its surface and the existing winds and fly later in the day or wait for increase in head wind or drain fuel to lighten the load if there are problems. Let's remind ourselves for the moment about density altitude, although it is touched on in the Mountain Flying chapter, too.

If you are at Grand Canyon 6605 feet elevation and instead of standard temperature of 38 degrees F, you have 100 degrees F, your density altitude is more than 10,000 feet. More fantastically, if you are taking off from Bryce Canyon, Utah, with 7586 MSL and it's not the standard temperature of 32 degrees but

110 degrees, your density altitude is more than 12,000 feet. Let us look at one of the most popular family aircraft ever built, the Cessna 172, and study its performance on takeoff.

At sea level on takeoff, the Cessna 172 requires 1525 feet to clear a 50 foot obstacle. 2500 feet above sea level, this distance increases by 385 feet; go up another 2500 feet and now the extra increase is the first 385 feet plus another 570 feet. At 7500 feet above sea level, the 50 foot obstacle distance on takeoff is 1525 feet + 385 + 570 + 1375 feet; i.e., the increments themselves increase greatly with altitude. At 7500 foot elevation, you need 3855 feet of takeoff distance instead of the sea level figure of 1525 feet. But if your temperature outside were 80 degrees instead of the standard 32 degrees, you would need by Denalt Computer 3.2 times the sea level figure or 4875 feet. This is all relevant because many desert trips are both hot and high. They also are often dirt or soft field and that adds another 7% or 340 feet. This means that if you are taking off at 7500 mean sea level at 80 degrees F, you need 5215 feet for a 50 foot obstacle *if* your C 172 is brand new and flown by a professional pilot who is as sharp as a tack. Remember, the sea level distance was 1525 feet.

The Denalt Computer, incidentally, tells us that your rate of climb will be 25% of your sea level climb at this 80 degree 7500 foot altitude air strip. Even though those are *my* figures, I've astounded myself with those figures. We truly have to keep reminding ourselves of the significance of density altitude. Humidity also alters the picture. We all remember from our student pilot days that moist air has less lift, but we forget that very hot air has increased capacity for carrying moisture and may be more humid than we realize.

During your preflight you will naturally have windows and doors open for cooling, but make sure the plane's contents are secure as desert winds can make a map or hat disappear faster than a jackrabbit.

Don't load your passengers too soon unless you want to see your supply of water used up prematurely. 190 degrees F has been recorded on the seat of a jeep at Imperial Valley Navy Station in California during World War II and that is hot enough to roast pork in your oven. File your flight plan and ask local pilots for advice if you have questions about terrain or your ability.

During taxi, watch the wind sock and hold the correct aileron as dust devils are common. If you see one of those miniature twisters heading for you, turn to face it; don't underestimate this danger. If you are on a rough strip with gravel, do some of your pre-takeoff check while taxiing to avoid gravel and propeller damage while stationary. During your run up, face into the wind and keep it brief. On sand, consider omitting the carburetor heat check to avoid soiling your engine with unfiltered air. Remember to recheck cowl flaps and to lean engine for best mixture prior to takeoff. Many veterans, if using a notch of flaps on rough strips, will not pop the flaps down until just prior to rotation in an attempt to reduce flap damage by stones. Don't be in a hurry to rotate and get airborne, as mushing off in a half stall has caused about 100 accidents a year to general aviation planes for many a year.

Monitor the oil temperature gauges and cylinder head temperature during your climb and change to cruise climb as soon as possible. Be aware and not alarmed by sluggish performance in hot humid days at altitude. If you find a thermal, make like a glider pilot and enjoy it to gain altitude. Get your heading nailed down early as it is easy to get lost over featureless terrain and Lawrence of Arabia you ain't.

Cruise is always cooler at altitude in flying the desert; it is often smoother there and pilotage is facilitated if you are high enough to see the land properly. VOR reception is better. Remember, too, that the charts you are consulting for your cruise performance should be those for your cruise density altitude, not your true

Retain your altitude over remote terrain, watch your gauges for engine warnings, carry plenty fuel, then enjoy God's gift to a Nation where the Green River joins the Colorado.

Photo: A. E. Turner, Utah Travel Council

Keep your thumb on the map, watch the clock and hold a heading. Painted Desert, Arizona.

Photo Credit: U.S. Dept. of the Interior, National Park Service and the Wilderness Society

height above sea level. In other words, if your altimeter says 5000 feet in flight but instead of standard temperature of 41 degrees F, you have an O.A.T. of 81 degrees F, you'd better take your cruise performance data from the 7500 altitude column. This sure stops pilots from doing buzz jobs near the ground; I've missed many excellent desert photographs by not wanting to sacrifice altitude which had been gained in hard fashion the way a miser attains riches.

Desert cross countries require some foresight with weather. They should be planned early or late in the day when it is cooler and to avoid summer thunderstorms. The desert air is usually dry but sudden storms will follow cumulonimbus buildup around noon and often persist until late in the day. The storms are usually easily seen and can be circumnavigated but you only need one day of dodging storms and being rattled by the bone-jarring turbulence to make you a believer in early starts. I have personally found sunrise so bright and warm in the American Southwest that I am up early and more able to go than I am dragging along on a dreary, dull day in the Northeast. The days seem longer, too. Severe winds and wind shifts are the mark of the desert also and I recall in two biographies of pilots, their amazement on flying east across the mid Atlantic to Dakar, Africa, to find sand storms 300 miles west of West Africa over the open sea. Miniature twisters are very common in summer, moving across the desert floor, and should be watched for carefully during taxi and loading. The excellent visibility causes confusion in navigation . . . you see your checkpoint but it never seems to come up. The rule of thumb is guess your distance, then multiply by a factor of three for the correct figure. I have embarrassed myself several times by calling in my position prior to landing and being well out with my data. Once I called Roswell, New Mexico, "Landing five minutes," and actually took 20. Had to

If you are flying low over desert terrain, expect turbulence and remember density altitude is a feature of heat as well as height.
Photo Credit: FAA Aviation News

fake it, told the tower operator I stopped to change a flat tire, but he didn't believe me.

Thermals are common in the desert and are useful phenomena if you are laboring on takeoff. If suddenly you get one during your cross country, accept it gracefully and don't complain when you get the corresponding drop later to balance things.

Donald Bower calls the desert "a land of superlatives . . . the geographical giant," but looking below at the terrain, you are more likely to be struck by the brown, drab emptiness of what is below you. Now you will find many dune buggy trails crossing our desert, giving a false impression of civilization. There are many mesas also which look like large aircraft carriers. Surely, you think, for an emergency landing you could easily slip down on to the table top with no subsequent problems. Wa-aa-ll, it's been done with fatal results. A landing on a flat mesa may be a technical success, leaving the pilot no way to descend vertical walls. They once found a mail pilot in the late

1920's frozen to death two miles from his plane in Utah. He had been unable to get down from his landing site, although the plane was later fueled up and flown off.

Try to carry in your head a constantly up-dated picture of the nearest settlement, creek or landmark. Stay oriented. Know where you are. My old sectionals of Utah, Arizona and Nevada are full of pencil notations with the time-over recorded at the checkpoint. Those marks form the basis for reconstructing your position if you ever get . . . here comes the four letter word . . . lost. I hotly defended those marks once against a snickering pilot friend until he pointed out that some of the times showed I was flying in a circle (he says, but damned if I'll admit it!). The ability to hold a heading, to mark time over your last checkpoint and to keep a thumb on the map is a prime necessity in flying any featureless terrain like desert.

You probably should navigate by established airways or follow railroads or roads. If you come down, you want to be

A course bracketed by a river is a navigational reassurance in any rugged terrain.

Photo Credit: Michael Anderson

where other pilots will be routinely flying and the smart guys don't often fly direct. You can keep track of your position more readily if you remember a mile in 60 seconds is 60 miles an hour; a mile in 40 seconds is 90 miles an hour. Moving up into average cruise speeds, a mile in 35 seconds means you are doing 103 miles per hour, 30 seconds equals 120 miles per hour, 25 seconds equals 144 miles per hour and 1 mile in 20 seconds equals 180 miles per hour. Therefore, if your checkpoints are marked off along your route in increments or units of a number of miles, ground speed can be more readily calculated. Monitor 121.5 occasionally as you cross a desolate area and, for your own protection, carry extra fuel and top up every chance you get.

Prior to landing, try to get surface winds at your destination as some of the fields are dangerous one way strips and you want to know in advance when you land uphill if you will also be with the wind behind you. If the strip is not one way and go around is possible, don't be afraid to make your first circuit of the pattern a go around. You can assess ground conditions well this way and improve your subsequent approach. One seasoned pilot suggests setting up your landing configuration high on the approach, then doing a go around watching how much altitude you lose in the thin desert air before you get tidied up. This figure, for example 300 feet, then becomes the critical distance in your next approach, i.e., once 300 feet above the ground, you are committed to the landing.

Remember to fly by the indicated air speed and not by your impression of ground speed; carry a touch of power on final as there is a tendency to undershoot due to thin air with poor lift and due to the illusion in clear visibility that you are closer to the threshold than you really are. Be prepared despite the faster sink rate for chaos if you hit a thermal and watch the wind sock, your drift and the ground for dust devils. (Question: Margaret, what's a dust devil? Answer: Something

Write down your time over any checkpoint and know where you are at all times in the desert.
Photo Credit: Utah Travel Council

Over popular scenic attractions, expect to find other tourist pilots flying the outdoors and keep your neck twisting. Badlands.   *Photo Credit: Travel Division, South Dakota Dept. of Highways*

swept below the carpet!).

Taxi to your parking spot, flying the plane all the time, and try to get a grass site for parking as it is cooler. Listen to 121.5 again to prove that you haven't activated your own ELT by your landing, then tie down very securely. You may wish to leave a window open if there is no vandalism problem as radios and plastic computers take badly to those extremes. You may not wish to top off until you know the density altitudes at the time of your departure. If you top off to avoid condensation, you may lose some gas as it expands. You should, however, refill your water containers if you have been snitching some from your survival kit during the flight.

Emergency landings in the desert are made easier by your awareness of where the dirt roads and civilization are and your constant appreciation of wind direction. Dried up lakes may offer a landing spot but if they are too brown, they may be wet and a poor landing surface. The edge may be firmer and distance above the surface is easier to estimate at the perimeter due to landscape contrast. Leave your wheels down as you can lose a lot of your forward momentum by sacrificing your gear against rocks, and as always, fly the plane to the last at its slowest speed.

It is interesting, even frightening, to read the advice of desert survival experts who point out that the desert sun can kill you in a few hours, but with their help, you can stay alive for a *few* days. Edward Abbey may call the desert "the most beautiful place on earth," but there are plenty of bleached bones out there that have disagreed.

One of the earliest survival stories is that of Sven Hedin who attempted in 1894 to cross Asia from west to east. He finally survived the East Turkestan desert of Takla Makan only by resting by day buried naked to the neck in sand with his clothes above as an awning. This is the first lesson: nothing is hotter than the desert surface. The Seattle Institute for Survival found in one situation that where the surface was 147 degrees, the temperature was 110 degrees six inches down and 79 degrees twelve inches below ground level. If you cannot dig down, then elevate yourself off the desert; it is appreciably cooler one foot above the ground than on it.

How much heat can man stand? Well, he is relatively frail and enjoys only a five degree range of 97 degrees to 102 degrees body temperature. Doctor Craigh Taylor was the first to experiment with heat tolerance and once accepted an exposure unprotected to 250 degrees F for fifteen minutes. In Washington, wearing a protected thermal suit, a volunteer tolerated 970 degrees F for 90 seconds!

In 1960, survival experiments in the Arizona desert at 120 degrees F in the shade temperatures showed that

(1) You can acclimatize to heat in one week if you do light work only; and

(2) All "furious activity" had to be forbidden, with duties being tackled only gradually.

The first rule we find, therefore, is get out of that bloody hot sun and stay motionless. Dig a hole under the aircraft, get into it and cover your head. Wait until sundown before doing anything more.

Usually man loses about five pints a day in sweat, urine and breathing; and dehydration will ensue unless this fluid loss is replaced. The second rule emerges—find and drink water. When you lose 2½% of your water weight you start to feel unwell and have difficulty being rational. A loss of 10% may be the start of the end although some athletes can lose 15% in contrast to camels and desert snails which can sweat out 25% of their body weight.

The Mexican trapper Pablo Valencia added to the folklore of the Southwest Arizona desert when, in 1905, he traveled on foot 150 miles in 90 degrees F shade for eight days without water. He lost one quarter of his body weight but recovered in a few hours.

For most people trapped in the desert,

Ancient lake deposits form an intricate erosion pattern in Death Valley. If this is your emergency landing site, then cinch your seat harness and fly the plane to the end.
Photo Credit: U.S. Dept. of the Interior, National Park Services and The Wilderness Society

HANDY TIPS

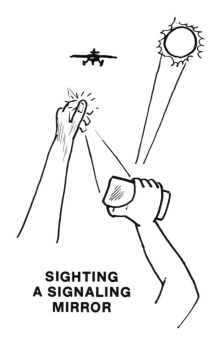

**SIGHTING
A SIGNALING
MIRROR**

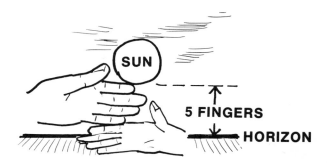

**15 MINUTES PER FINGER
TO SUNDOWN**

e.g. 5 Fingers
= 5 x 15 Mins.
=1¼ Hrs. to
Sundown

5 FINGERS

HORIZON

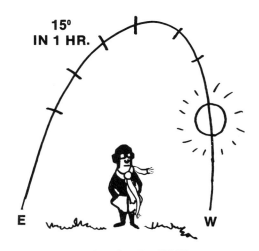

15°
IN 1 HR.

E

W

**SUN MOVEMENT
15° IN 1 HOUR
1° IN 4 MINS.**

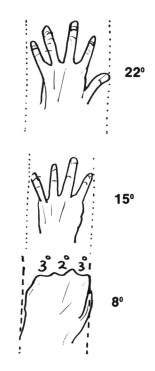

22°

15°

3° 2° 3°

8°

**How to judge degrees
of an arc**

a loss of 10% causes so much tongue swelling that death will follow unless the body is cooled as the mouth may become too dry to swallow water. S A S parachutist Jack Sillito found this out in 1942 when he was stranded in the Libyan desert. He walked 180 miles in eight days without food and little water. He saw three jeeps but had no saliva to shout; he set fire to his shirt but his signal was not noticed. He finally followed the jeep tracks back to safety, losing from 182 pounds to a weight of 112 pounds.

Water is the prime necessity of the desert. If you have one quart, you'll live three days if you rest and don't move; with one quart, you'll live two days if you travel by night, then rest when exhausted. How far might you get? Well, despite Valencia and Sillito, you cannot hope for more than 40 miles in two days if you are lucky and on flat, firm ground. Each year, 23,900 cubic miles of water fall on the Earth, but don't count on any in the desert.

If you have water, drink it. It is the water in your body, not the water in your canteen, that saves your life. If you have no water, wait until it is cooler in the evening and forage for it. Tim Kneeland, a desert survival expert, suggests that a hot weather survival kit should contain a few old white bed sheets. The Arabs really know their terrain, and their most suitable garments can be fabricated from white cloths. Cover your head and body. If you don't have a head cover, make a kerchief from the tail of your shirt and use it for a hat. Space blankets make excellent reflectors of heat during the day and preserve warmth during the chill of the desert night.

If your survival kit contains material for a solar still, you can set that up after sundown or in the early morning when it is cool. Do not attempt to dig one during the heat of the day as you will sweat more water loss building it than your still will produce as replacement. Your still, under ideal conditions, may give you a pint of water every three to four hours. Your

chance of finding water by digging in low areas or where you find vegetation is not very good but when it's cool, you may try. In salty areas, don't dig too deep as fresh water is lighter than salt water and stays on top in any pool that is tapped. Flies, ants, bees and grain eating birds can often show the way to water and animals' spoor marks may lead you to water holes. Beware of any pools which lack animal marks or fail to grow vegetation, as arsenic contamination can occur in the United States deserts. You may be able to collect dew on piles of stones in the morning. If there is any dew, you can tie rags or tufts of grass to your legs and walk through any foliage to pick up fluid which you then squeeze from your rags. You can chop up and mash cactus pulp (gloves and a machette are useful in a desert survival kit) or try to tap vine and tree roots. You must get water—remember the Utah family with their desert automobile breakdown. They survived on the water in the car radiator.

Food is not so important, but all moving things can be eaten, even lizards. Snake meat tastes like "chicken, tuna, veal, frog, rabbit" to different people. You can get one pound of meat on a four foot rattler and two and a half pounds on a five foot one.

To sum up your desert situation so far, the advice is: stay with your plane but don't stay inside it because of its furnace-like hot contents. Get in the shade down in the sand until it's the cooler evening. Drink water without rationing, try to build up a supply of water. Don't talk, keep your mouth closed to decrease water loss.

Once organized, you can prepare your signals using as many methods as you can think of. You are almost always best to wait with the plane. You are underestimating the distance to help and overestimating your fitness to reach it.

If you decide to walk out, follow the discussion in a previous chapter. Collect a water supply before you go and travel only at night. If a sandstorm overcomes you, lie down in the direction of travel. Use lots of Chap Stick or zinc oxide cream on your face and lips, though engine oil may help. Wear sunglasses or make something as a substitute. Go around deep gullies rather than through them and don't walk without direction or purpose. Hold a heading. Don't lose members by striding out too fast but go at the speed of the slowest member. Stay together as even a poet knows more about it than we do. I quote William Stafford's poem *In the Desert*; "What is that stiff figure moving oddly out in the sun alone?"

For further reading, we suggest a free pamphlet which requires 30 cents postage: *Desert Survival,* published by Maricopa County Department of Civil Defense, 2035 North 52nd Street, Phoenix, Arizona 85008.

WATER REQUIREMENT CHARTS
(from "The Physiology of Man in the Desert" by Adolph & Associates

(A) NUMBER OF DAYS OF EXPECTED SURVIVAL IN THE DESERT, NO WALKING AT ALL:

Available water per man,

U.S. Quarts	0	1	2	4	10	20
Max. daily shade temp. F				Days of expected survival		
120 degrees	2	2	2	2.5	3	4.5
110	3	3	3.5	4	5	7
100	5	5.5	6	7	9.5	13.5
90	7	8	9	10.5	15	23
80	9	10	11	13	19	29
70	10	11	12	14	20.5	32
60	10	11	12	14	21	32
50	10	11	12	14.5	21	32

(B) NUMBER OF DAYS OF EXPECTED SURVIVAL IN THE DESERT, WALKING AT NIGHT UNTIL EXHAUSTED AND RESTING THEREAFTER:

Available water per man,

U.S. Quarts	0	1	2	4	10	20
Max. daily shade temp. F				Days of expected survival		
120 degrees	1	2	2	2.5	3	
110	2	2	2.5	3	3.5	
100	3	3.5	3.5	4.5	5.5	
90	5	5.5	5.5	6.5	8	
80	7	7.5	8	9.5	11.5	
70	7.5	8	9	10.5	13.5	
60	8	8.5	9	11	14	
50	8	8.5	9	11	14	

The importance of temperature reduction to the survivor is highlighted by the following in Chart A: Temperature 120 degrees, water available 2 quarts, days of expected survival 2; reduce the temperature to 100 degrees and 2 quarts of water will extend your life expectancy THREE TIMES.

This importance to a potential "survivor" cannot be overemphasized.

Night travel, or better, NO TRAVEL, is stressed.

6

MOUNTAIN FLYING

"To the timid traveler, fresh from . . the lowlands, these high ways, however picturesque and grand, seem terribly forbidding — cold, dead, gloomy gashes in the bones of the mountains, and of all Nature's ways the ones to be most cautiously avoided."
                    JOHN MUIR
                    born 1838 Scotland

MOUNTAIN FLYING

Mountains are seen differently by different people. The old Maine farmer turned down the offer to buy from the artist who had raved about the view with the comment, "danged fool—nothing to see but a few rocks and those danged mountains." And yet they have such majesty, such grandeur that mountains are climbed for the ultimate experience by the nature lover. For poor Mallory and Irvine climbing Everest in 1924 "because it was there," it was, of course, exactly that—the ultimate experience. Hawthorne referred to mountains as "earth's undying monuments," a concept felt by the early Indians in our nation. When Darby Field of Exeter, New Hampshire, climbed 6288 foot high Mount Washington in my State in 1642 only two Indian guides would accompany him since the "Great Spirit would eat them at the top."

Well, if you don't want the Great Spirit to eat you at the top, you have a lot to learn about mountain flying. Fortunately, the subject is about the most popular of all flying discussions and there is no shortage of reading material to improve your skills. Many of the western states have free pamphlets on the technique of flying in their state, and they have safety counsellors available to help transient flatlanders. Again, asking local pilots for advice is a sound investment but be sure to ask *pilots* as residents of Jackson Hole, Wyoming, are reputed to say, "Ain't no reason to climb mountains if you ain't lost nothing up there."

Writer John Boynton states that there are for the pilot "two mandatory areas of study: mountain weather and the capability of the aircraft he will use." The poets add their comments. Peter Abbott says, know the "tortured terrain and the devilish sky above it." Howard Snyder reminds us that "man is only a temporary and uninvited intruder." Ernest Thompson Seton describes the land below as "sordid meanness" and Lord Tennyson, the poet, I hope describing the eagle and not me the pilot, says, "he watches from his mountain walls, and like a thunderbolt he falls . . ." Enough of the poetry, on to the prosaic, well, maybe just one cute quotation of pilot Don Dwiggins, "a mountain is something to avoid . . . look, don't touch."

Let's go fly the mountains with many experienced fliers, learned writers and wistful sad eyed search and rescue pilots. As it's man and machine against the mountains, let us first look at homo hopefully sapiens.

The pilot is probably the key to everything. He has to have something more than solid bone between his ears. But it is more than that. It is not intelligence or knowledge or even wisdom that he needs. He must be patient and have certain personal rules, especially if he is a transient flatlander; rules like no night flying and no IFR in the mountains. He must also be cautious as he can turn a friend's weekend into instant fun or permanent Hell. Mountain pilot and Bonanza owner, Jerry Coigny, declares that high country pilots "who can't find a way to go over or around (rocks) just have to forget it until another day."

Jeff Morrison of Helena, Montana, adds also that the pilot should exhibit "understanding" and make intelligent decisions on the ground in preflight rather than flustered alternatives in the air.

The pilot should also show a kind of reverence or at least respect for the high terrain. Perhaps his attitude on the ground is as important as the attitude of the aircraft in flight. Certainly the three peaks of human error in a pilot's professional life occur when he is at his most blase toward the risks of general aviation

Be aware of your aircraft performance at density altitude to avoid fatal surprises.

Photo Credit: Cessna Aircraft Company

flying. Attitude is more significant than experience or skills. Respect for high country is demonstrated by the true mountain man, and even Edmund Hillary on top of Everest in 1953 found himself studying the unclimbed peak Makalu 27,790 feet high, below him, and in deference wondering if there might not also be a way of scaling it.

The pilot should have comfortable skill with the sectional map and pilotage should be a recently practiced art. He should have prepared for the high thin air by, in practice, taking off with reduced power, and stalls and simulated landings at high altitude should have demonstrated to him how sharp the stall is in less dense air, and how almost uncomfortable minimum controllable speed is at altitude. He should have nailed down flying by the numbers. Faster than usual approaches, and unusual unconventional approaches could be practiced with an instructor with the pilot going to full flaps and a slower approach speed just before the threshold. This technique is only a bit different from that required by high traffic density towers of pilots on fast finals.

The pilot and his passengers should be dressed for the terrain below, with special reference to boots and windcheaters. The pilot's health should be good. He should not suffer from any health problem which could be increased by altitude such as anemia, emphysema or recurrent heart problems. The rules about alcohol are especially important in the high terrain; and as for smoking, when are all you dingbats going to get the message? Doctors aren't particularly clever (ask any CFI who has tried to teach one) and if 100,000 physicians out of 250,000 total in the U.S.A. have given up smoking in the last 10 years, why can't you huffers and puffers catch on? — Sorry, end of sermon.

I landed once in Jackson Hole, Wyoming, to find the local pilots a bit unimpressed by my oxygen kit. They felt that they could get almost anywhere by pilotage without oxygen, but they were acclimatized to altitude and more tolerant of any oxygen deficit than tran-

Large bodies of water form excellent checkpoints and help your non-pilot passengers to understand map reading and pilotage. Flaming Gorge Lake.   *Photo Credit: Utah Travel Council*

Often low lying clouds simulate distant lakes to confuse your navigation in the mountains.
Photo Credit: E. G. Anderson

sients. Their amusement at the cautious ingenue didn't bother me—even at sea level as a student pilot I was conning my CFI that my bad landings were due to hypoxia.

The high terrain is no environment though for the pilot who cons himself. To fly the mountains, first know thyself. There are many flatlanders walking around who have made poor judgments in weather in the East but says Bud Corban, there are few mountain pilots who "walk away from bad decisions in mountain weather."

The plane should be as well-tuned as the pilot. When you look around at FBO aircraft at high altitude strips, you may find chips on the paint, but the engine will be perfect. I once took some dual mountain instruction with Clinton Aviation at Arapahoe County Airport, Englewood, Colorado, and found their maintenance impressive. They, of course, don't touch the Cessna 150, the standard workhorse of the East; the Cessna 172 with full fuel and only two aboard is their standard training plane. They point out to their students, that the only thing an aircraft does well at altitude is sink. They remind their pilots about weight and balance in the mountains and point out the dangers of being overgross; their statement is that mountain pilots are usually honest: "You can't fly an excuse." The need for runway length is altered by a decrease in weight by a factor of two; for example, decrease the weight of the aircraft by 3% and the runway length need reduces by 6%, cut the load by 8% and your runway can be 16% less. In these days of inflation, that's an impressive gain.

Know the numbers for the plane you are using, no—not just the inside pages of the Owner's Manual—but show a familiarity with the machine that is almost indecent. Know the maneuvering speed at different weights remembering that it decreases as weight decreases. You should know your expected rate of climb at different altitudes and translate this into how many feet per mile on takeoff. A measurement then of distance from airport to your highest en route terrain clearance will give you the practicality of what you are attempting to do. You should even know the time in seconds that you normally take to get airborne, and a little bell should ring inside your head when you start to go well beyond that time on takeoff. How many miles do you need to do a normal or steep 180 at cruise speed because your mountain visibility should be at least three times that? As Richard Collins, the editor for *Flying* magazine, says, if you don't know the numbers for your aircraft, "stay in the Great Plains until you do."

The effect of density altitude is covered in Desert Flying where it was discussed to remind the reader that heat is as important as height. Density altitude is such a common bedfellow in high terrain that high performance aircraft are much to be preferred. Let us take a moment to tabulate the different performances of the Cessna 172 with its big brother Cessna 182. This is why you see so many 182's, Bonanzas and Cherokee 6's in the mountains. Incidentally, most local pilots say you should not consider IFR mountain flying unless your aircraft can climb readily to 18,000 feet mean sea level. In fact, IFR skills are not the answer to the high country. Most aircraft flying mountains should manage close to a climb of 200 feet per minute at 15,000 feet to be considered safe mountain aircraft.

COMPARISON C 172 with C 182

	C 172 feet/minute	C 182 feet/minute
Rate of Climb 10,000 feet MSL gross	230	445
15,000 MSL gross	20	220
Gallons used from sea level	11.5	11.5
20,000 feet MSL 2500 lbs. = 900 lbs. above empty weight	0	105
Service ceiling	13,100 feet	17,700 feet

Weather is the next consideration and is covered in simple but explicit detail in the excellent AOPA *Mountain Flying Course* booklet (c) 1970, AOPA Air Safety Foundation (Ken Hoffman and Bill Stanberry).

If you ask AOPA's Flight Planning Department, they will also send you terrain flying reprints from their magazine *Pilot*.

Mountain weather is one of the four main U.S.A. weather types; the others being, Coastal, Gulf and Plains. Experience in one area is not necessarily helpful in another as it's a new ball game. Mountain weather is characterized by weather stations which are far apart with data which may be dated by the time you eyeball it yourself in the air. Pireps older than an hour are similarly limited in value as mountain weather is often fast changing, going from IFR to CAVU in 12 hours. In fact, Richard Collins reports that CAP pilots often find a wreck in such fine

weather that it is obvious to all that a moment of patient delay by the pilot would have prevented the accident since 90% of all forced landings in the mountains are weather crashes. Mountains are weather factories creating many storms within major systems, frequently with weather being IFR one side of a pass and splendid VFR on the other. Heat and density altitude play their part also. There are some flights which had no chance even on paper due to density altitude. Just as the kid from next door cycling past without using his hands is "an accident going somewhere to happen," so there are some mountain crashes which were almost planned to occur.

Wind is weather. Walter Boener, production test pilot for Beech Aircraft Corporation and former Rocky Mountain pilot with experience of the Swiss Alps and the South American Andes, is quoted as stressing that the Central Rocky Mountain area is "the worst spot in the whole

Fly the upwind side of any ridge; it has the lift and the smoother air. Hell's Canyon.
Photo Credit: Idaho Dept. of Commerce and Development

world for downdrafts." The wind in the American mountains can be like a monster firehose wielded by a giant fire department. Manufactured by those winds and terrain are downdrafts of unparalleled ferocity, and pilots should never fly where they are counting on lift from the terrain to give ground clearance (although some CAP Piper Cubs are flown almost like gliders by SAR personnel). Accident counsellors, who should be used and believed by any flatlander, point out that *light* winds over a ridge may be more of a surprise to the approaching pilot as the downdrafts are more subtle and deceptive and don't hit until the plane is only 500 feet from the ridge.

Come and chew some tobacco or dip some snuff with local pilot mountain men: "Plan to keep some room between you and the ground!" "Small mountains are just as hard as big ones." "Go around a mountain and not through it." "You're an awfully long time dead!"Anyone else to be quoted? Here's Richard Collins again, and although he is too articulate to be put amongst the mountain men, he does point out that on the slopes of the Rockies, careless pilots are aluminum litterbugs. Dave Boles, a Boulder, Colorado, CFI and co-author of *Mountain Flying for Lightplane Pilots* (c) 1970 General Avia-

tion Series, says the "easiest way to make mountain flying safe is to keep out of the mountains as much as possible." True, and accidents happen every month where the pilot doing a dog leg arrives and a direct route flier never ever shows up. But mountains *are* part of our wilderness resource and man is uplifted (literally) on seeing them and you do hear "I am closer to God on my mountain than I am in my church"—leastwise, that was always the excuse of my father-in-law, Bob Hunter. Why fly mountains, is a bit like the situation when Willie Sutton, the bank robber, was arrested. "Why rob banks, Willie?" the police asked, to receive Willie's explanation, "because that's where the money is!" Why fly mountains? Perhaps we've done a 180 and come back again to George Leigh-Mallory and Andrew Irvine, but Rudyard Kipling said it also:

"something hidden — go and find it
 Go and look behind the Ranges."

Wind produces turbulence, a dramatic description of which is given by St. Exupery in his writings of the Andes. Turbulence as mentioned in the desert flying chapter gradually develops and, once established, may well last until dusk. Flying early to give your passengers a smooth trip also pays off with reduced density altitude.

Intense winds at altitude can occur in

TURBULENCE INTENSITY

Class	What Happens	Airspeed Fluctuation in Knots
Light	May need seat belts	5 - 15
Moderate	Do need seat belts and passengers forced against them.	15 - 25
	Objects move.	
Severe	Plane at times out of control.	More than 25
	Objects thrown about.	
Extreme	Aircraft tossed about; practically impossible to control and structural damage may occur.	More than 25

the Rockies with formation of lenticular clouds in the lee of the ranges, and turbulence can be found more than 100 miles downwind in the plains. This mountain wave turbulence with secondary rotor waves and ground turbulence has caused many an unsuspecting pilot to remember that mountain flying is a surprise. Turbulence is so common that occupants of light aircraft should have their seat belts and shoulder harnesses fairly tight at all times, and gear should be battened, covered with a heavy blanket, and fastened with bungee rubber cords. The back shelf should be empty of IFR hoods and debris as once an automobile driver was killed in a sudden stop by an empty cigar box on his rear shelf.

In case turbulence is mentioned in pireps, you should have a clear picture of the classes of reported turbulence:

Of all the errors, and weird phenomena that you inflict on unsuspecting passengers, nothing will impress them, scare them or alienate them more than turbulence. Scares the pilot, too, especially if he's bald and not wearing a hard hat. On second thought, I think being in a night thunderstorm as a passenger in a light plane probably wins the dubious honor for fear.

Preflight has been partly covered in Desert Flying and some of the precautions of Winter Flying are also relevant. The pilot will have a sound weather briefing, and any optimism shown by the weathercasters will be treated with a grain of salt. You will be skeptical about cloud bases since they are seldom flat and often fall deeper into the valley or passes than the report would suggest. You will recall that weather can change fast. Almost every State Aeronautical Division in the West emphasizes not to fly if winds aloft at your altitude of flight are more than 25-30 knots. Find icing levels during your weather briefing, not suddenly later the hard way as descending to lose ice is not always possible in high terrain. Weather-related accidents in the mountains are a feature of the Appalachian chain, too, and the Pennsylvania Bureau of Aviation has a most active, busy Safety Division which gradually is removing the label

Attain altitude on takeoff by circling over the airport before crossing any mountain range. Don't cross any ridge while still climbing. Photo Credit: Idaho Dept. of Commerce and Development

86

"Hell's Stretch" from the Alleghenies, mountains which are a significant aviation hazard in the East, but which flown correctly should not stop the tourist from enjoying the beauties of western Pennsylvania.

If your source of weather information is limited, place your long distance call for more data as it's your life we're talking about.

Don't chase omni stations during your flight. VHF radio is line of sight and for proper reception, your altitude on Victors airways may have you at your service ceiling. Dog leg if it is safer to do so, as it is better to follow recognizable pilotage features like roads or railways, than head over terrain that contains dragons and fiery serpents that will eat you up. Dead reckoning doesn't work too well in the mountains due to capricious winds. If you are following a road or railway line, watch out for tunnels, which will leave you high but maybe not dry. File a flight plan—adding the word flares to it if you are carrying pyrotechnics. If you deviate at all from this flight plan, be sure and modify it from the air. If for some reason you cannot file a flight plan, be sure and tell a friend or the FBO of your flight intentions.

Compute density altitude and takeoff requirements from the Denalt Computer and the assessment of wind, runway surface and slope and if in doubt, wait until it is cooler. The old Koch Chart, though inaccurate, was a more dramatic presentation and a pilot had to be pretty obtuse not to get the message of pressure altitude corrected for non-standard temperatures. If density altitude is high, you may be able to take off with minimal fuel provided you can gas up at a better nearby airport; if you don't have the self-discipline to gas up elsewhere after takeoff, you will be breaching another of the rules of mountain flying: carry extra fuel in case weather or head winds make you look for an alternate and 50% extra fuel is not too much at that.

Go to the owner's manual if necessary for a decision on flaps for takeoff. The surrounding terrain and local pilots will have indicated whether departure downhill and downwind is preferred. Be ready for cross winds and turbulence or uneven ground, and don't expect ground effect to be so useful in the thinner air. As you rotate, you will be glad your center of gravity is not too far aft as this has been a common cause of stall takeoff accidents.

For takeoff, have the mixture leaned as required and get to your best rate of climb speed or best angle depending on departure considerations, and hold it there. Don't cruise, climb. Know your best rate and angle speeds with the variation imposed by altitude increments. Some authorities recommend climbing 20-30 miles per hour faster than stall speed if there are many sudden up drafts which could easily stall a wing on takeoff. You should certainly circle over the airport to gain altitude before crossing peaks; to attempt a ridge crossing while still climbing is folly. I once attempted to fly over the Little Big Horn Mountains after takeoff from Sheridan, Wyoming. My astonishment at failing to reach altitude that hot day before reaching the peak could easily have been prevented by a moment's consideration on the ground with a measuring ruler and knowing the rate of climb in feet per mile for that density altitude and loaded aircraft. This is important as one writer points out that "some valley floors can outclimb Wichita."

If you are caught by density altitude at takeoff, don't mush along in a half stall but fly by the numbers, and like a glider pilot look for lift from wind and terrain or fly downhill. Inability of an airplane to perform due to heat, height and humidity is independent of airplane type or pilot experience. Every plane has been caught, even the high powered ones. To single out any one aircraft is unfair unless we point out that all manufacturers' products were designed for best performance at sea level. The Mooney Mark 20 F, an excellent machine and I would love to have one, figured a few years back in two

Try to get at least 2000 feet clearance flying over any mountainous terrain and be ready for downdrafts.
Photo Credit: Cessna Aircraft Company

Verify that your rate of climb can handle the speed with which the terrain is rising. Use your artificial horizon, not the tops of peaks to avoid the false horizon trap.
Photo Credit: Idaho Dept. of Commerce and Development

episodes to show that pilot experience doesn't cause or solve mountain flying problems. In 1972, a 43-year-old private pilot with about 150 hours experience was killed on takeoff near San Diego due to uncalculated density altitude; in 1969, a CAP pilot, same age but with five times the experience, was killed by density altitude in a canyon in a flaming crash in the Sierra Nevadas on an S A R flight. It *can* happen to you; you *can't* fly the mountains the way an experienced truck driver rolls along the interstate highway; you *can't* be switched off any time your plane is switched on and flying the high country.

You're finally in cruise — great. Bet you thought we'd never stop talking to let you get on with it. So far, so good. Visibility is excellent due to the dry, clear air. The gauges are being watched closely because engines don't suddenly quit— there is usually some instrument prewarning. You are listening to weather and asking for any pireps. When you have a moment, you switch to 121.5 to listen to any ELT or other pilot signal. You lean the mixture more as you climb, and you notice again your relatively poor rate of climb at altitude. Your speed is satisfactory because you know air speed as well as altitude is like money in the bank.

You've achieved a height 2000 feet above any mountains you'll be crossing, and you recall Richard Collins' concept that perhaps you shouldn't tackle any mountain route more than 75% of your service ceiling. You are prepared for turbulence with tight seat belts, but I hope not tight expressions, and should it become a problem, you will be down to your maneuvering speed in a twinkle. You are ready for downdrafts and determined not to blaspheme and further scare your passengers when it happens.

In a down draft, you'll add power, put your nose down and go to maneuvering speed to get out of the down draft with the greatest dispatch. You will be coordinated in turns at altitude because the thin air stalls the wings so much more

easily than at sea level.

You are remembering as you fly some of the classic problems of high terrain. You know about false horizon or lost horizon where the tops of peaks are, in error, taken as the horizon rather than the mountain bases; and you check with your air speed indicator and artificial horizon to prevent that trap.

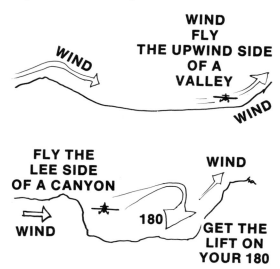

You have been taught about ridge flying by the accident counsellor and know to cross at a 45 degree angle rather than head on, in order that you can retreat with a 90 degree turn which is faster than a 180 degree turn should you meet a down draft you can't handle. Since the sink is on the lee of the ridge, you are especially alert if you are flying upwind to cross a ridge. Look down at the tree line as you cross any ridge to confirm wind direction from any trees. Look beyond the ridge to see if the other side is rising up to show itself, a sure sign that you are crossing with adequate height. Be prepared for the corresponding updraft less you inadvertently enter the bases of any low lying clouds.

What about canyons? I guess every flatlander has, in the movies, heard John Wayne holler, "head 'em off at the canyon," but many a pilot from the East wonders what in the bloody Hell *is* a box canyon? Good, maybe if you don't know exactly what they are, you will stay away

BOX CANYON

during your turn should you ever have to do a 180. One hears both sides of this argument. It makes sense to me to picture the flight on the lee side of the canyon; if you are flying there, you will soon know if the down draft is too much for you to fight and better to find out at the start of your flight when you have enough ground clearance than to find it to your horror during your turn.

As you approach any pass or canyon, circle before entering and study behind you for familiarity with your escape back—your out exit should you find a down draft. Are there clouds lying on the mountains and down into the pass? Is it clear, not just a hole in a lot of garbage but good solid VFR through and through? Know your chandelle or better your wing over turn should you get caught. Experienced mountain pilots "never commit themselves—they always have an out." Some also decry "imposed flight" over wilderness high terrain, but often for the tourist transient pilot, it's a *self*-imposed demand *he* puts on his machine. The

from them. A pass is a gap through the mountains, but a box canyon is an apparent pass which peters out at a higher elevation against the wall of mountain— it is rather like the space between two fingers which ends suddenly at the web. Many experts say fly the upwind side of the valley to get smooth air with uplift, but fly the lee side of a narrow canyon (if you must fly in canyons) to get the uplift

It is better to fly down a canyon and away from trouble than up to and into rising terrain.

Photo Credit: Beech Aircraft Corporation

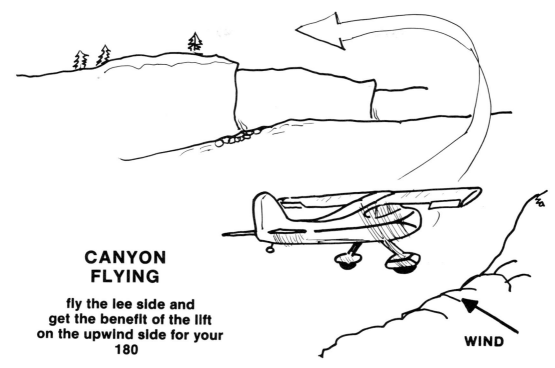

CANYON FLYING

**fly the lee side and
get the benefit of the lift
on the upwind side for your
180**

WIND

Mountains can be CAVU on one side and IFR on the other. Approach them with caution. "Three Sisters".
Photo Credit: Oregon State Highway Travel Section

plane would have been just as happy dog legging it by flatter ground, but nobody asked it for its opinion.

Well, we're almost there. We know the airstrip that is our destination because of prior study. It is not a one way strip, we know the runway surface is satisfactory and we are wondering about the safety of landing.

Anyone want to say something? Fred Arnell, a bush pilot in Alaska, does: "If everybody in the village turns out for your landing, don't land. Believe me, it works," as a prudent safety observation. In your let down, watch for excessive engine cooling and to protect ear drums, let down slowly. Your approach may be other than standard and may have to be chosen to suit the terrain. As you come in on final, maintain your best rate of climb speed at best lift flap setting, and hold a touch of power until you are committed to the landing. In this setting, you are ideally set up for a go around should the bottom drop out of things. Your approach speed will be faster but so is the stall speed in the thin air. In a tight pattern, you may have to slow down to facilitate maneuvering but, again, watch for that stall. Stay coordinated.

Be prepared for optical illusions with sloping runways. An upslope landing makes you feel you are high, and landing down a slope gives you visual stimuli that you are low.

Be prepared to buzz animals off the strip if it is remote and being used as a pasture. Consider wind direction and strength and anticipate turbulence, and be ready for weird noises on rough strips as you touch down. If unused to gravel, the noisy sounds can be quite alarming. Try to avoid one way strips which are sometimes better marked on the free

Know before you land, all the characteristics of your mountain destination airstrip. Is it uphill, one way, what are the approaches like and what do local pilots say about it?

(Photo Credit: FAA Aviation News

RUNWAY ILLUSIONS

State Aviation maps than the sectional ones. This is, again, data that you will pick up from local pilots better than from charts, AIM or the AOPA Airport Directory. If in doubt, flying over the strip may be of value, although the wind sock may not be of any help if planes land deliberately down wind but up slope. Try to spot aircraft both in landing or takeoff; otherwise you will be further confused. If on landing you find yourself rolling downhill too fast, take off and land carefully the other way. In winter, always check runway conditions at your destination.

FORCED LANDINGS IN HIGH TERRAIN

In 1912, Calbraith Rodgers, the first man to fly coast to coast, crashed in the

Wilderness terrain is below you at Juneau, Alaska even though the city is in sight. Be ready with your radio.
  Photo Credit: Alaskan Travel Division. Dept. of Economic Development and Planning

San Gorgonio Pass between Los Angeles and Phoenix. Since then, at least 12 other aircraft have fallen to the venturi effect of wind in this pass and their aircraft are painted with bright orange crosses to prevent a fatal rescue attempt by strangers. About 20 years later, Jimmy Doolittle streaked through the same pass on his way to the coast to coast speed record. Wrecks are scattered in the mountains as mute reminders of when man and machine challenged terrain and weather and were found wanting.

Ask the Civil Air Patrol what finds wrecks and they answer "great skill and great luck." Try to increase the chances of luck by making your forced landing where your plane will be seen. Turn down slope which may enable you to find an alpine meadow or at least better terrain. It also buys you time by giving you relative altitude above lower ground. As you run out of altitude, make a coordinated turn above stall speed upslope attempting to keep the wings level and go full flaps and land. Remember the change from your glide path to an upslope landing may be considerable and great back stick pressure may be required. Robert O'Hara, Commander of the CAP Squadron based below the San Gabriel Mountains, says, "Don't prolong the agony. When you know you are going down, make a controlled crash landing. Fly it all the way in!" Avoid lining up your aircraft nose and hence your own on a rock or tree. You should probably leave your gear down to expend energy, and, of course, your seat belt and shoulder harness will be well-cinched.

If you have a choice between a canyon or creek buried below you or a ridge in the open above the tree line, the latter will give you a more obvious location for aerial spotters to identify. Your ELT and radio will also work better there.

If your wreck starts to slide down the slope tail first with broken fuel tanks in the wings, in theory the spill will be left behind; whereas if you slide down nose

Minimum survival kit in the mountains: proper footwear, a mirror, a map and a compass — and Chap Stick.
Photo Credit: E. G. Anderson

first, the fuselage then drags through the gasoline with resultant fire risk to occupants.

You're safely down. "There is much comfort in high peaks, and a great easing of the heart" — Anon. You bet. Survival in the mountains may require enduring winter and desert climates and has been partly covered in those sections, but some words on mountain travel are not remiss. The going will be heavy, much more strenuous than you imagine. No, even more strenuous than that. One mile of traversing mountains is easily equal to two miles on the level—reminds me of the old Confucius joke, "never believe man on mountain, he not on level"; well, I said it was an old joke.

In cross country travel depending on your objective, travel up spurs since they then lead to the main crest but travel down streams since they all run into the main water courses. Be wary of streams because, snow fed, they are usually fast moving and very cold. Some mountain areas in the United States get an annual rainfall of 100-125 inches. ,

The military mountaineering groups have the slogan for cross country travel across slopes, "Never go uphill when you can go down. But never go down if it means you must later climb again." The intention is to conserve energy.

There is some danger in slopes of talus which is large loose rock, and scree, which is a smaller, looser formation. In traverse, let the lower foot take all the weight and use the upper just for balance—the hop skip method. Take short steps and keep away from big rocks. If a slide starts, run down with it but slant across and don't look down.

In climbing, keep your weight directly over your feet and place the soles of your feet flat on the ground even if it's sloping. Watch closely where you put your feet, and take small steps like an old man.

In descending, keep your back straight and knees bent with a Charlie Chaplin gait. Unless a slide starts, never run or you will end up with an ankle strain—a

major catastrophe in the mountains. Lean forward slightly. Face out if the going is easy, sideways if hard, and face in and pray if it is impossibly hard. At times, rest with your arms low as they will be as tired as if you have been boxing.

Natural shelters will be plentiful with caves and rock overhangs. If using a cave, use a fire to keep animals away and stay near the entrance. Check the rear dust for evidence of animal footrints or excreta as you may have company. Be sensible and rest. Paul Petzoldt, Director of the National Outdoor Leadership School, says, "At high altitude, a person can never afford to become overtired."

Despite the risks and challenges, flying the mountains remains a highlight of any light plane pilot's life, no matter where his home.

California may be Big Sur, Hollywood, San Francisco and Disneyland to many Eastern pilots, but it has its graveyards to flatlanders, too. In fact, one Sheriff's Squadron has a giant county map in its briefing room with the wrecks of 317 aircraft pinpointed on it.

The following discussion is quoted verbatim from *California Aeronautics Division* as yet another service it performs for its flying citizens. It is an ideal summary of "How To Fly The Mountains":

"Sometime you are going to take a trip which will require you to cross some pretty high country. The following advice will be of help to the amateur mountain pilot regardless of the number of hours tucked away beneath his flying belt.

1. First and foremost do not consider flying mountainous terrain unless you have at least 150 hours and are proficient in slow flight.
2. Know your airplane. Do not fly into mountain areas or land on mountain strips in an unfamiliar aircraft.
3. Remember that for each thousand feet you are above sea level, it will increase your takeoff run approximately 25% and your landing speed 2% with a longer run due to your increase

In mountain flying, know your winds aloft, ceilings, and highest terrain. If you don't have oxygen, be prepared to deviate via lower land. Direct VOR flying may not always be feasible or even desirable and remember omni reception is line of sight.   *Photo by Author; Kodalith by Dave's Studio*

in landing speed.

4. Know the field you are going into. Check with experienced mountain pilots if possible. Know the altitude, the length and whether it is a one-way field. Most of these fields are one way and on many it is impossible to go around if you overshoot.

5. Check your weather and stay out of doubtful or bad weather.

6. Make your trips in the early morning hours. The air, as a rule, begins to get bad around 10 A.M., grows steadily worse until about 4 P.M., then gradually improves until dark.

7. Stay out of the mountains if the wind is over 25 miles per hour.

8. Keep your airplane as light as possible. Do not carry one pound of needless weight. No aircraft performs at its best at full gross weight.

9. Route your trip over valleys whenever possible. Study your charts thoroughly—watch your compass and don't get lost.

10. Maintain as much altitude as possible at all times.

11. Hit all ridges at an angle so you can turn away if you hit a down draft. After you cross the ridge head directly away from it.

12. Expect the wind to be changing constantly in the mountains. Don't rely on cloud shadows for wind direction. If you can't gain altitude on one side of a canyon, try the other. If there is an improvement there, ride the center but under no circumstances head up any canyon or valley without sufficient altitude and room to turn around. The grade of the canyon may climb faster than your airplane.

13. Keep that flying speed in down drafts. Don't get panicky, just remember that air does not go through the ground. A ground cushion of air will always be there unless below the top of the timber. The stronger the down draft, the greater velocity it will have when it changes

direction.

14. Keep in mind that the actual horizon is near the base of the mountain. The mistake of using the summit of the peaks as the horizon will result in the aircraft being placed in an attitude of constant climb and may inadvertently lead to a stall. Remember you will not have a horizon to check the attitude of your plane once you begin to let down in the mountains. Watch your airspeed and your altimeter.

15. On landings, come in upstream whenever possible and with the airplane at minimum speed with power. If the plane is settling too fast add more power. If it is not coming down fast enough cut a little power—but do not make power off approaches— They Are Dangerous! When you are sure you will hit the runway near the end, chop the power and make a full stall landing. These mountain strips are Short.

16. Use common sense on takeoffs. If the air is bad or if you have a tail wind, wait it out. Remember none of these fields are long enough to land again once you have left the ground. Let the airplane use all the runway it needs as long as runway is available, then it will be flying when it leaves the ground. Do not pull it off until you are sure of flying speed, unless you run out of runway.

17. You can gain extra takeoff speed by making your turn at the end of the field at a good fast taxi speed and opening your throttle as the plane swings around to line up with the runway. Practice the maneuver with an instructor on a good standard airport.

18. Before you fly into mountainous terrain, practice short field landings with power, upwind, downwind and crosswind. Be sure you can set your plane down on a 50 foot spot, not once in awhile, but every time.

19. Do not fly into any basins or valleys at high altitude that do not have an outlet where you can get out in a hurry in case of down drafts.

20. Remember winds of from forty miles per hour and up are common at 10,000 feet altitude.

21. Carry enough gas to make your complete round trip plus 50% more. You will need it more times than not.

22. Take maps with you. Know your route and weather.

23. File a flight plan. Let someone know when you are going, the route you are going to use, and when you will be back.

24. Fly the airplane every second, don't let it fly you. You cannot make mistakes in this territory.

"Under ordinary circumstances you can expect the wind to be blowing upstream in the mornings and afternoons, as the air and terrain heats up, and downstream in the evenings as it cools off. Cold air is heavy and goes down hill while hot air is light and goes up. Expect to find down drafts over all streams as they cool the air. Know the wind if possible; watch the topography and with a little common sense you can tell where the updrafts and down drafts will be. Remember air is like water and follows the contour of the land it is flowing over. Use the updrafts to help you gain altitude but do not fly a ship in this territory that does not have a ceiling sufficient to get you out without help from the updrafts.

"Always remember that you are flying in a huge and very sparsely populated territory. If you have an accident, it may be some time before anyone knows about it. Carry an emergency survival kit. In the event of a forced landing, stay with the plane. You will be landing on fields where there is no one to help you in case of trouble and it is a long walk out. Don't take chances and don't get rattled.

"Use your head and eyes—the best airborne computer around."

As the poet Anne Sexton says,
"These are the warnings . . .
   if you're climbing out of yourself
   If you're going to smash into the sky."

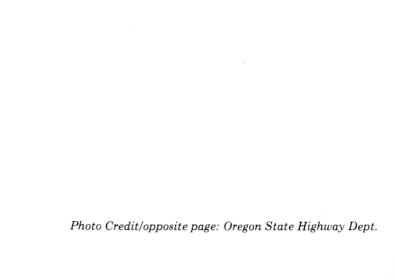

7

FROZEN
TERRAIN
FLYING

"Frosty air sets our blood to racing"
EDWIN WAY TEALE

FROZEN TERRAIN FLYING

Frosty air does more than that. A pilot who parachuted into the Alaskan wilderness in thin clothing died of exposure before he hit the ground due to heat loss from the wind chill factor. How cold is cold? Let us look at what Author Nicholas Monsarrat wore in 1941 on convoy duty in the North Atlantic: "Two vests, thick long pants, third best uniform trousers, big clumping sea-boots, a sweater and a fisherman's jersey, a duffle coat, a towel and a woolen scarf around my neck, sheepskin gloves . . . a Balaclava helmet and in addition a long curly beard." *Breaking In–Breaking Out* (c) 1966 Wm. Morrow & Company, Inc., New York.

Frozen wastes are a challenge: crisp sharp visibility and excellent engine performance balanced against the vagaries of weather and the vulnerability of the shut down engine and the cold weather start. For many pilots, it is more than a challenge, it is a way of life. The lore of the Arctic is that of oil drained before it freezes and numb fingers holding a plumber's firepot in attempt to thaw an engine for routine travel, and it is from Alaska, Siberia and the frozen Poles that much aviation cold weather knowledge has accumulated. Even although you don't intend to fly any further north than Moose Jaw, you can benefit in northern state winter flying by lessons learned from land, sea and air in more severe climates. Tales of the sea first warn us of such climatic severity. Consider Henry Stone in 1850 when the H.M.S. Investigator was caught in icebergs "such a deafening grinding that you could not hear a man speak unless he put his mouth to your ear and howled into it." Consider Lt. Rhodes in 1884 finding two men in the shipwrecked City of Columbus, "both had frozen to death in the ratlines," or when the Larchmont was wrecked in 1907, "Purser Young was rescued with his body completely encased in ice."

Man is actually more tolerant of cold than heat although either can surely kill him. Man can harden himself to sleep naked at an air temperature of 50 degrees F, but, in fact, there is a case on file— surely a record—where two Pennsylvania hunters survived except for their toes a *body* temperature of 58 degrees F. This was when Wise and Lantsberry endured part of the winter of 1961 frozen solid in a hut when carbon monoxide fumes made them too weak to move. Your aircraft is less tolerant than man. Let us turn to consider pilot and plane in cold weather flying.

How are you, the pilot? Does cold bother you? Do you suffer from any affliction that is worsened by cold? Have you ever had frostbite or swelling due to cold? Do you have circulation problems like angina or Raynaud's disease? Do you have musculoskeletal problems like bursitis or chest problems like bronchitis or asthma?

Wear sensible clothes in layers and peel off if you heat up to avoid sweating and chilling. Pilot Gordon Sherley recommends flannelette pajamas as ideal underwear (No, Margaret, a shortie nightie is not the same), and advises any pilot to refuse seats to any passenger traveling in the Arctic who does not have adequate clothing as "the American North probably offers the most challenging flying in the world." Ideally, outer garments should not cause static and should not be synthetic fabric; but in practice, winter wear is so uniformly of that material, that most pilots use nylon outerwear and simply exercise diligent caution when refueling. Gloves are desirable and if dexterity is required can be of thin nylon or even the cotton ones seen in photography shops. Don't touch cold metal with bare fingers or you will leave more than fingerprints as many a cold weather camera buff has found. Avoid propeller blast as this introduces the wind chill factor. Ideally, you should have a parka with a hood but this limits visibility around frigid airports causing many ground accidents. Every winter, I treat in a New England emergency room, pedestrians who have walked into automobile traffic for the same reason. As usual, have an appropriate survival kit close at hand to grab if you have to leave the plane in a hurry. This is not an idle thought. In frozen wastelands it may take nothing more complicated than a flat tire or a dead battery to create a survival situation. A rolled up parka, with gloves and a spare pair of sunglasses in a pocket, should be stuffed under each occupied seat and Chap Stick should also be carried.

What about your plane? Well, there's more to it all than just removing the wheelpants. Perhaps you should try to arrange for the annual to fall in the late autumn so the plane can put its best foot forward for winter. Have proper insulation around fuel and oil lines and use the correct oil viscosity. Have the electrical systems checked, the control cables and your heating system also as carbon monoxide accidents are essentially winter ones. Check your windshield defroster before the need arises and remember that gyros tolerate cold badly as frozen bellows take time to work. Your avionics suffer as much in cold moist air as they do in the heat of the desert and should be checked out while your aircraft is being annualled. This is the time also to review your owner's manual with reference to winterization, and to have your winter engine baffles fitted if this is advised. Baffles increase the engine compartment temperature by about 50 degrees F and should not be fitted if your winter weather is intermittent. I used to own half a 1958 Cessna 175 which, during our New

Alaska from the air. Surely here even the most slothful would carry a survival kit.

Photo Credit: The Wilderness Society

Hampshire "February thaw" gave problems with engine overheating because of baffles and the FAA is on record as stating that you are probably safer without adding winter baffles if your airplane lacks a cylinder head temperature gauge. Your tool kit should include a small whisk broom to brush out of the cabin snow brought in by feet, and a brush with a small handle to remove snow from wings.

If you intend to carry Thermos jugs with you, remember all the horror stories about the pressure release of containers at altitude . . . "pilot blinded" . . . "instruments ruined in sudden IFR cloud of coffee" . . . etc.

Tires are a story in themselves. Discussions on nitrogen and antifreeze in the tires are beyond the scope of this book or the flying done by most winter enthusiasts. Inflation, however, is a more practical point as tire pressure rises and falls about 1-3%, depending on which tire manufacturer you believe, for every 5 degree F change. Under certain extremes, if flying into very cold from warm climates, you may wish to leave from the sunny South with overinflated tires. The tire companies don't officially favor this concept but allow that "modest overinflation won't hurt and may improve bead seal." Make sure you keep the same tire pressure on both sides and that tread depth is also equal, because on ice you need the best.

If your plane is in cold storage in a snow region, your investment justifies a weekly visit. Snow should be brushed off when it is still powder and not left until it is a kind of frozen Hell. You should pull the propeller through with the usual precautions and push the aircraft slightly forward or back onto a different part of the tire to avoid permanent flat spots. Make sure the brakes are not left on during winter. It is much more fun to fly your plane carefully through the winter than to have cold storage problems, but one of the (few) joys I now have as a renter pilot in the Northeast rather than an owner, is

not looking to the sky for snow and cursing twenty times a year as I drive to the airport with a brush.

Each Fall, trailer and camper owners remove their batteries and store them in a warm basement, showing that they are smarter than pilots. Come to think of it, some pilots don't even know where the battery is in their plane. When did you last check yours, or your ELT for that matter?

Winter flying makes such demands on the battery that we should consider this for a moment unless you have the more expensive nickel cadmium battery which also has its AD's. Lead sulphuric acid batteries tolerate cold badly, as any northern state motorist knows. A fully charged battery will produce 100% cranking output only at 80 degrees F. At 32 degrees F the output is down to 65% and at 0 degrees F (32 degrees of frost) the output is less than 40%. This shows the value of both going into winter with a freshly charged battery and of preheat on very cold days. If the electrical load to turn an engine at 0 degrees F is 250% of that needed at 80 degrees, the result is often a dead battery and dead batteries freeze at 0 degrees F, although a fully charged battery will not freeze until −95 degrees F. Bill Bassett, a Corporate maintenance chief in Fairbanks, Alaska, cycles his companies' batteries "every 30 days without fail."

Let us follow through on a frozen wastes flight and learn from the mistakes of others.

Weather is the first consideration and even for local flying, the pilot needs to have current data. Winter brings its own problems. My grandfather George Thom with his creaking bones used to say, "Winter don't come by itself, winter don't come easy." Boy — he knew!

Winter weather is characterized by long nights with correspondingly reduced daylight hours. At sundown, there is a definite chill in the air with runway problems at airports. Runway lights may be buried in snow and not visible from the air; and, in fact, if it is a small strip you are visiting, the FBO may go home with the sun, leaving you en route with no data regarding your destination. A telephone call to your destination from 2-3 hours out is always of value especially if you are flying into the snow belt. Refer particularly to runway conditions. Is he plowed out, what is braking surface like, what is the field temperature and dew point? Be prepared to find your destination closed and your alternate necessary. Be wary of reports from the tower as to runway conditions if it is reporting opinions on braking from recently landed airline jets. Airline pilots are thought by many to underestimate the severity of icy conditions on landing as it is alleged a too honest report on braking action would close down traffic too often.

Winter weather also is dominated by many small storms with rapidly changing weather rather than large fronts with prolonged stable situations. Cloud bases tend to be lower causing more IFR traffic; and fog, freezing rain and en route icing become problems. A plane taking off from a warmed hangar into a snow storm will melt snow it climbs through until the wings have cooled enough to ice up, and this happens often enough to be a cause of winter accidents. Remember, too, if you are flying safely in subzero weather and choose to apply carburetor heat, you may increase your temperature enough to bring it into the ice range.

Strangely, there is less snow in the Arctic than our Northern states as the lack of moisture keeps snowfall light. Although the climate in the "Flying North" is variable, in general it is marked by cold winds, which increase wind chill and cause large snow drifts. The Arctic spring and fall are seasons of rapid change with fog which decreases visibility, increases snow blindness risk and reduces by moisture the insulation value of clothing. Summertime brings an unbearable insect season and head nets and repellent should also be part of your survival kit. The Arctic winter gives long nights of no sun for six months, long twilight and moonlight off the snow giving, at times, 100 miles of visibility. If you get stranded in the Arctic, don't think it is just like the desert and that you can dig down for a more reasonable climate; the permafrost goes down for 900 feet in some places.

You've checked weather and stopped in at the FBO or any corporate pilot office for local advice or information. One seasoned traveller says that no matter how much it surprises you, *always* believe local pilots in difficult terrain.

Preflight is often hastened if conditions are miserable and passengers frozen, but this is exactly when an even more careful examination is required before you venture off. It is best accomplished in a heated hangar. Exaggerate how long it will take and your passengers will be pleasantly surprised if time is shorter. If you are parked outside, try not to load your people until ready as they can steam up the cabin within minutes.

The windshield should be de-iced if necessary but take care as many of the abrasive compounds and devices suitable for glass on a car will ruin a plastic windshield. Compounds containing isopropyl alcohol are usually safe. Later, you will want to turn on cabin heat and the windshield defroster prior to takeoff to purge the system of any moist air which would suddenly make you IFR on takeoff and also because a heated pliable windshield will tolerate gravel or even bird strikes better than a frozen rigid one.

All orifices should be checked (reads like a list for a physical examination!) as ice can be stuck in pitot tube, gas vents, exhaust and air intake and static ports. Verify that the air vent on the gas cap is patent also.

Cables should be tested, and any extra unusual control lock which you use only in winter should be remembered. All control surfaces should move freely, brakes should not be jammed, and the trim tab should not be frozen.

Drain holes should be tested and fuel drained once regularly and again. The problem of ice in the fuel which melts later to cause stoppage is a real problem and probably the only solution is to drain your fuel every chance you get, even if you land only for coffee. You might have to de-ice radio antennae.

Getting ice or snow off the wings is a must. Snow should be brushed off but for very adherent ice you have to either use a heated hangar or wait for the sun to come up. Either way, it is going to take hours and you may as well just accept it. Studies by the FAA showed that materials like teflon, silicone and polyurethane did not have any anti-icing properties by themselves, although they made it easier to release ice from aluminum. How many pilots have grumbled at the tenacity with which ice clings to aluminum? Well, the FAA have measured this as a force of 200 pounds per square inch, and for once talking a language that we mortals can understand, have explained that this is "the force exerted by the end of the trunk of a one ton elephant adhering in flight to the underside of an aircraft wing." Therefore, with a high wing aircraft, get up on those steps and survey the top of the wing as even one quarter of an inch of frost can be fatal. Planes with T tails require a close look also. As they say at the ski resort airfields, "listen to us or on takeoff you'll put a big sitzmark in the snow!"

Some takeoff accidents have been attributed to ice within the aileron causing flutter and loss of control. If this odd sensation appears during winter flight, reduce speed and land.

Icing equipment should be evaluated during the preflight as pneumatic boots can be damaged over the year by clumsy attendants, ozone and ultra violet radiation.

This is a long tedious preflight, it is cold, you are in a hurry to go and your passengers are complaining. Experienced winter pilots say you don't need to do those extras. You can always "up your insurance"!

Before starting up, you should review your owner's manual for cold starts. Read up on handling ground fires. Learn the nuisance of frosted plugs and overpriming. Consider asking for an auxiliary power unit start if temperatures are very low. Charges for an APU are really very reasonable when you consider that with a low battery, you may not be going anywhere. It is like the question to Maurice Chevalier, "Sir, how do you like being 80?", and the flashing smile answer, "It's better than the alternative!" Watch the temperature gauges carefully and know from your manual what is acceptable.

Taxi very slowly avoiding deep snow, slush or ice puddles. Don't turn fast in the cold as you can break the seal on tubeless tires. Watch out for hazards buried in snow especially if your plane is low wing. In general, avoid braking, although in very cold climes some people drag their brakes to warm them and the tires.

Run up watching the gauges closely, and check all positions of the fuel selector in case one tank has a frozen fuel line. Give it enough time to show up; perhaps taxi on one tank and do the run up on the other, then switch back and give it a bit longer to block on you. Allow adequate time as it is never a good idea to take off on a tank that has not been adequately checked. AOPA points out that all this warming up and fussing may consume as much as 10% of your fuel so watch your needs closely. Your oil temperature and pressure gauges should be moving into the green now and if some congealed engine oil allowed a pressure rise it will not have been a sustained one, and your last glance as you set your DG with the runway should be to verify that oil pressure has not dropped back to the peg.

On takeoff, choose dry portions of the runway and if there's any crosswind, start on the upwind side of the runway in the expectation that you will be blown downwind during your run. Be gentle with the throttle as you have a power increase due to the opposite of density altitude. I have taken off at Manchester,

New Hampshire, 200 feet MSL with a temperature of −12 degrees F, which gives a 6% boost to takeoff power, enough to blow off a cylinder head. Because of this "lower density altitude," the fuel air ratio may be too lean, to create other problems. Be ready for anything with a winter takeoff. A few years ago at a nearby strip in New Hampshire, a CFI salesman took off with an M.D. customer and family. As the prospective buyer rotated, apparently the frozen air intake became blocked and the engine quit a few hundred feet over the end of the runway. The pilot was given no chance to turn and spin in, as the CFI shouted, "I've got it," and crashed safely straight ahead in a frozen marsh. The first few minutes of the winter takeoff command attention!

Engine overheat in the climb may be due to this power over-boost or just the obstruction of your winter baffles. If the temperatures are going up, climb faster and open your cowl flaps. Gear should be left down a bit longer to drain off water and the gear should be cycled several times to dry it. Test all control surfaces and trim tab settings in any climb through moist air.

You are now settled on your cross country cruise. Keep tuned into weather and open a flight plan if appropriate. Know which airports on your route are open for fuel and which are open summers only. Don't run one tank completely dry as you may wish to return to it if the new tank has frozen fuel lines. Watch for power loss which means pull carburetor heat, and keep an eye on your temperature gauges because if they are running low maybe you should get a winterization kit for your engine. Be attentive to headache or confusion and suspect carbon monoxide poisoning if you feel unwell; a carbon monoxide detection kit is not perfect but it is better than nothing. If it is really cold outside, cycle your gear and prop at intervals. Are you holding your heading, because pilotage is not so easy when the ground is blanketed with snow. Lakes in particular disappear,

the contours of rivers change and only railway lines and occasional interstate highways appear to be in their correct locations.

The subject of icing en route is well covered almost any winter in every flying magazine, and since poor old Don Jonz perished in Alaska after his article "Ice Without Fear" in *Flying*, October 1972, I will superstitiously leave the discussion to others; besides, what the Hell do I know about IFR icing?

The let down phase may see excessive engine chilling. Pull on carburetor heat before you reduce power and close your cowl flaps early. Open your throttle often during your glide and be ready to drop your gear and flaps early in order that you can carry more power on the approach. Be ready for a forced landing if your engine quits as you will probably not be able to start it again.

Landing can present problems for many reasons. Often snow is plowed to the threshold and heaped in a bank which merges with the surrounding snow-covered terrain. Don't drag in low over the numbers as you may clip your gear on an unseen snowbank. A pilot did just that at a strip 20 miles from me last winter. Yet do not come in hot and high because there may be poor braking on the runway which requires you to land short and slow. Try not to use brakes, and in crosswinds as in takeoff, go for the upwind side of the runway. Keep your nose wheel high as it will tend to stick in the snow with sudden nosedown compression and damage. By the way, land on the runway. One poor pilot in Maine, two years ago, thought the snow piled in a long rectangular pattern beside the runway was, in fact, the runway and his aircraft still had its tail sticking up in the air when I landed there in the Spring.

If there is unbroken snow with no shadows, be prepared for whiteouts especially if there is fog or poor visibility. Even as experienced a pilot as Max Conrad crashed dramatically at the South Pole due to this phenomenon. Paul

Woods, the Safety Officer for the Flying Physicians Association, points out that the first winter landing of the season may be difficult "because your depth perception changes, due to lack of clues that you are used to seeing in summer and spring conditions." If your brakes or gear are frozen and the wheels don't rotate on landing, a flat tire may well result.

After landing, again taxi slowly, and at a strange airport try to park where experienced local pilots choose to tie down. Check the gauges and allow the engine to run at about 1000 RPM for one minute before switching off. Check your tires for cuts if they are over-inflated and you have landed on gravel strips. Fill your fuel tanks but if you are doing it yourself, verify there is no dirt or snow in the end of the fuel nozzle. Even if you are wearing anti-static clothing, be careful not to spill fuel as ice may prevent proper grounding of the plane and cold brings fuel into its critical flash point temperature.

If you are landing on ice, don't if the temperature is above 4.4 degrees C. However, if you have freezing temperatures, seven inches of fresh water ice or fourteen inches of sea water ice will allow a 3000-pound plane to land. A 5000-pound aircraft needs nine inches fresh water ice or eighteen inches sea water ice. White ice on top is only one half as strong as the clear ice below. The ice should be twice as thick if you are parking overnight and don't put the weight of your airplane too close to that of other aircraft.

What if you have to come down as an emergency in frozen wastes? Will you be able to hack it? Remember 26-year-old Augustine Courtnauld in the 1930 British Arctic Air Route Expedition, exploring the air route to Canada by the great circle passage. He existed as a weather volunteer for the five months of winter in a six foot high, nine foot diameter tent with outside temperatures at 8000 feet MSL of −60 degrees and winds at 100 miles per hour which puts him off the wind chill graph at equivalent −148 degrees F. His fuel ran low and on a restricted diet, he lay mostly in the dark "not a dog or even a mosquito for company . . . the silence was almost terrible. Nothing to hear but one's heart beating and the blood ticking in one's veins." Relieved in May 1931, he was out hunting ptarmigan within five days!

Since wind chill is so important, we will print below the table that is demonstrated in almost every book on flying or camping:

An *emergency landing* over frozen terrain presents several problems. Altitude may be hard to estimate unless trees or manmade landmarks can be seen and size judged. Wind direction may not be obvious and you may land downwind without realizing it. Whiteout is likely and certainly judgment of the height at which to flare can be as difficult as a glassy water seaplane landing. A frozen lake may be available, in which case try to land near the edge to judge altitude from trees. Again, approach above stall speed and be prepared for the nose to dig in as you suddenly slow in deep snow. You can expect to go over on your back with fixed gear in deep soft snow and gear up may be your choice under certain circumstances with retractable gear aircraft. Remember, too, with conventional landings in airports that the windsock may be frozen and showing the wrong wind direction.

Don't stay in your aircraft wreck in cold weather as the metal may conduct away your body heat fatally overnight in sub-zero weather.

As always, your first consideration is shelter. If time is limited, make the simplest protection you can, then get into it. Don't work at such a pace that you start to sweat because moisture in your clothing reduces insulation whether it is from melted snow, rain, sweat or accidental wetting in streams. Wet clothes are extremely hard to dry in cold snow country.

If you have a tent, it should be pitched promptly after you stamp out a flat platform in the snow. Try to get the snow

THE WIND CHILL FACTOR

Wind Speed (mph)	Actual Temperature (F)											
	50	40	30	20	10	0	−10	−20	−30	−40	−50	−60
	Equivalent Temperature (F)											
0	50	40	30	20	10	0	−10	−20	−30	−40	−50	−60
5	48	37	27	16	6	−5	−15	−26	−36	−47	−57	−68
10	40	28	16	4	−9	−21	−33	−46	−58	−70	−83	−95
15	36	22	9	−5	−18	−36	−45	−58	−72	−85	−99	−112
20	32	18	4	−10	−25	−39	−53	−67	−82	−96	−110	−124
25	30	16	0	−15	−29	−44	−59	−74	−88	−104	−118	−133
30	28	13	−2	−18	−33	−48	−63	−79	−94	−109	−125	−140
35	27	11	−4	−20	−35	−49	−67	−82	−98	−113	−129	−145
40	26	10	−6	−21	−37	−53	−69	−85	−100	−116	−132	−148

(Wind speeds greater than 40 mph have little additional effect)

LITTLE DANGER FOR PROPERLY CLOTHED PERSON	INCREASING DANGER	GREATER DANGER
	DANGER FROM FREEZING OF EXPOSED FLESH	

To use the chart: estimated or actual wind speed, left-hand column; the actual temperature in degrees F top row: The equivalent temperature is found where these two intersect.
Example: with wind speed of 10 mph and temperature −10 F, the equivalent temperature is −33 F. This lies within area of "increasing danger of frostbite" and protective measures should be taken.

level and flat, as it will freeze the way you have it with any bump in it a solid protuberance. You can't use tent pegs the usual way in ice but you can chip out a hole, then set the pegs in with water which will freeze. More likely with snow, you will use a long branch or thin log as a "dead man's support." The branch buried in the snow alongside the wall of the tent can have the guy ropes around it, and if the knots are kept above the snow line, the ropes may be pulled through when you leave. Stake the upwind side of the tent first for obvious reasons. In setting up camp, be cautious with glacier-like streams, as a trickle of water may become a torrent of melting ice as the day warms up.

As you work, pay attention to wind strength and if wind chill is increasing use what shelter you have as quickly as possible. There are no rules about building snow shelters, and as Raymond Bridge

SNOW CAMPING

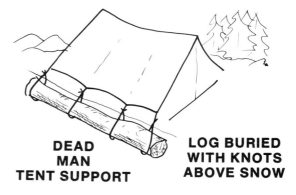

DEAD MAN TENT SUPPORT

LOG BURIED WITH KNOTS ABOVE SNOW

points out, "the main ingredient . . . is ingenuity." Snow, because it contains air, has some insulation properties and is, in fact, a benefit not a hazard in winter survival.

The simplest shelter is to burrow a hole in a snowdrift or snowbank and if you are wearing thick good winter clothing, simply enter your hole until the storm is over or until morning comes. However, cold air sinks so don't sleep too deep in any snowhole. A fallen tree or tangle of roots or brush may have a natural snow cover over it or you may be able to fell a tree by cutting it part way through above the ground, then pulling it down to ground level on the broken hinge of wood which is left.

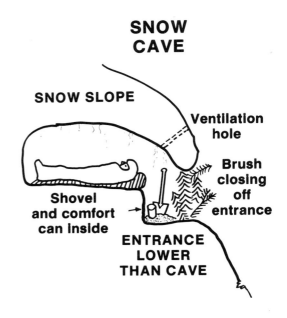

SNOW CAVE

SNOW SLOPE

Ventilation hole

Brush closing off entrance

Shovel and comfort can inside

ENTRANCE LOWER THAN CAVE

SNOW HOLLOW

FIRE

SNOW HOLLOW SURVIVAL

Tree hollows make excellent temporary protection. They are the scooped out areas at the base of trees. You can enlarge one side for sleeping and on the other side, build a fire which may require a roof to protect against melted snow from the branches.

If wood is plentiful, a lean-to can be constructed; or if snow is reasonably compacted or consolidated, you can dig down a hole almost like a coffin (omigosh, he's flipped!) and build up walls to form a hole igloo.

Finally, if you can find a steep slope of snow, a snow cave can be constructed. Make it as small as possible and have the inner sleeping area higher than the entrance to allow cold air or melted snow to escape. Use seat cushions from the aircraft to insulate the floor and seal the entrance, but be sure to bring some kind of digging tool into the cave with you. An air hole should be punched out with a long branch, especially if you are going to use a stove inside the cave. Don't build in the lee of any slope as winds may give you a mammoth digging out problem after any subsequent storm. It is better to have the wind blowing across the entrance or even slightly into it. With snow shelters, there is the problem of adequate ventilation to prevent carbon monoxide poisoning if you have a fire or stove going. As the inner walls ice up, oxygen does not penetrate into the chamber as it does through snow and this ice has to be chipped off. If it is not cold enough for snow construction, there is condensation and melting with subsequent problems with clothing. Remember, too, to keep out a urinal or can with a lid for nature calls.

Hypothermia has already been considered in a previous chapter, but don't forget how you may insulate your feet and clothing by using moss, grass, stuffing of seat covers or other fabric from the plane. Make extra outer shoes using burlap or plane carpet and if you are not exerting yourself and sweating, plastic bags can be used between sock layers to form a barrier to heat loss. In our New England winters, mothers often put their children's feet into empty plastic bread bags to augment the insulation of socks. Boots will have to be taken into the sleeping bags through the night or they will be too frozen in the morning to wear. What sleeping bag? Jeez, you don't mean you were dumb enough to fly over frozen terrain without one (if so, I don't want your money for this book. Just go. Go. Well, you *can* pay your money but don't expect us to like you.) Most survival experts accept as criminal, winter terrain flying without proper clothes, sleeping bags and several methods of starting fire. If a snowmobile can drive you in a half hour farther than you can walk out alive, imagine what a plane can do.

Fire starting can be a problem with wet wood, but usually enough squaw wood (the dead small lower branches still on the trees) is available. If you are above the timber line, your choice is basic. You either carry a stove or eat uncooked food. Don't eat a lot of food at bedtime as it diverts food from the skin to the stomach and chills you.

At night, move around in your sleeping bag as if you were boxing or bicycling. Get the circulation going before you fall asleep. Don't cover your mouth inside the sleeping bag as you will dampen the sleeping bag contents. Smear Chap Stick over your lips at bedtime.

Again comes the question of travel or stay put. The factors have to be considered again. Thin or solid consolidated snow may be easy to travel on, but deep soft snow requires skis or snow shoes. These articles of snow footwear can be improvised, however, from aircraft parts or trees. How far are you from anywhere? Do they know you are out there? Flight plan? Are you fit or injured? What survival kit do you have? Has your ELT gone off? Do you have radio contact?

Snow trench. Snow is actually an asset in any winter survival situation. The shovel handy inside the cave is a necessity in case of wall collapse.   *Photo Credit: Rocky Mountain National Park*

Rescuers or rescued — the going is tough for both. Dress for the terrain you overfly.

Photo Credit: FAA Aviation News

Bush flying in the Arctic has legendary tales of those who've stumbled back alive, for example — Eielson, Wilkins; those who were found dead after stumbling — Gillam; and those skilled in ice and snow who were never found — Don Jonz.

Which will you choose, especially when there are similar legendary tales of those found and saved who never left their wreck site?

If you decide to travel, be attentive to your direction. Don't rely on finding your tracks if you have to return, but look back frequently and note landmarks on a homemade map. Use your compass, and in varying snow conditions, change the route to utilize compacted snow or areas where there are no drifts. Don't exhaust your strongest man by constantly using him as trail breaker, since you may need his skills later. Don't split up to find different trails, especially in any storm. Watch out for frequent wind changes, whiteouts and snow storms and don't try to travel if the weather worsens but stop

and dig in.

In winter travel, study which slopes get the sun as this may contribute to avalanche danger and the weakening of any natural snow bridges. Take care with cornices where wind-driven overhanging snow slopes on ridges are a risk to the traveller.

Be cautious approaching banks of streams as snow may be undercut by the water and if you fall and freeze, you may die.

Ice travel may be the easiest but think back to the start of winter. Was there a lot of cold weather before snow fell which usually gives solid ice, or did snow fall a lot in early winter to insulate water from subsequent freezing? In very cold weather, lake travel may be ideal but river ice is almost always suspicious, especially in the spring. Walk on the inside of river curves as the ice on the outside of the curve may have been eroded by the river current.

Stay away from rocks that protrude

WINTER TRAVEL

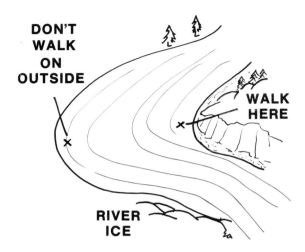

DON'T WALK ON OUTSIDE

WALK HERE

RIVER ICE

through the ice. Have your party widely spaced, roped, and carry a long pole to probe and have a knife handy to use as an ice ax if you go through.

If you feel the ice cracking, fall forwards or sideways on your chest and stretch your arms out into a cross. Try not to jackknife into a vertical position as that increases the strain on the weak ice. Crawl away, don't stand. If the ice is too thin, and you go through, expect the sudden shock of cold to numb and exhaust you and cause panic. There are about 200 deaths a year in the United States due to ice accidents. Survival times depend on water temperature and it is said that winter North Atlantic convoys in World War II did not stop for "Man Overboard" as statistics showed he would be dead of exposure within minutes. If the ice is too thin, break it away with one hand, sup-

porting yourself with the other, and attempt to work your way to shore or stronger ice. Remember, one inch of ice will support small animals; two inches of ice will support a human adult; but three to four inches will give better support. Clear transparent honeycombed ice is unsafe and solid ice has a blue sheen or color to it. You should stay off ice during the noon sun thaw, and never gather in groups or build a fire on ice.

If you are a rescuer, have a rope around you and lie on the ice, don't stand. Extend a long object, with hands as a last resort. A human chain can be formed. If you dive in to rescue, don't expect to see your hole unless you are within two feet of it. It is a fallacy that there is air between water and ice, and the Red Cross always warns against the "fatal rescue."

For first aid, if you can maintain a source of heat for the victim, warm him up fast. If all you have are blankets, use them without otherwise warming the patient.

It is beginning to look as if staying put with the aircraft makes sense. One survival expert carries a small bottle of champagne in his aircraft survival kit to celebrate his beating the odds in an emergency landing. Hopefully, he will not use it in winter as Calvin Rutsrum states that a survivor who "drinks in the winter wilderness runs about the same risk as a man who drinks and drives."

For further reading, the reader is referred to *Snow Camping Guide,* Raymond Bridge, (c) Charles Scribner's Sons, New York.

"The primal fear . . . meeting that dark wall of the wooded swamps of North America . . ."
JOHN MITCHELL

8

FLYING THE WETLANDS AND SWAMPS

FLYING THE WETLANDS AND SWAMPS

Talking to a mountain man — fantastic; chatting with a desert traveler — great; where do you find a swamp man? To most of us, the wetlands, tidewaters and marshes of our country are unexplored and that is the way to leave it as you overfly such terrain. Many experienced cross country pilots would just as soon come down in any other wilderness as a swamp, and for good reason.

Who needs company, who needs wildcats, bears, panthers, alligators, crocodiles, deer, otter, manatees — yes, manatees, what's manatees, I don't know, look it up, here it is, they are sea cows. Who needs herons, wild turkeys, ibis, egrets and the roseate spoonbill? What about ahinga, pelican, tortoise, wild hog, bald eagle, cormorant, woodstork, lynx, snake, lizard and toad?

Who wants to live amongst all that? "Life first drifted in shallow waters," said Rachel Carson, but we'll settle for life with Man not creatures. You prefer Man, really? The first private warden hired by the National Audubon Society to protect the egret in 1905 was murdered by poachers. That's Man for you.

Take care as you fly the wetlands that you don't get murdered also by the unique problems of the "dynamic ecosystem" below you. Plenty of other fliers have succumbed: In 1930, there were 1½ million wading birds in the Everglades; in 1940, 300,000; and in 1950, 50,000. In the same year, 1950, there were 100,000 woodstorks; in 1965, 5500 and in 1970, 3000. Things with wings can perish in the swamps — so learn.

Try to skirt swampy areas if possible—the time spent is better than the eternity if you don't.
Photo Credit: Cessna Aircraft Company

Advice on surviving in our wetlands can be obtained from any National Park Ranger in the Okefenokee Swamp of 341,000 acres in Georgia or the Everglades Park which encompasses 1,400,533 acres in a 5,000 square mile swamp. If you are flying over or past 5,000 square miles of featureless primeval swamp, certain needs or requirements must be met similar to those for crossing any desert. Previous chapters have covered the salient points in detail. The plane should be well-maintained and carry maximum oil and fuel, weather briefings obtained, navigation details attended to and a careful heading maintained. Pilotage from a sectional chart is probably impossible for newcomers. Check the DG against compass frequently. Be attentive for any bird strike and buzz the National Park System at your own peril. The Department of the Interior has, in fact, sued private pilots under the Airborne Hunting Act for "using an aircraft to harass birds." Fines up to $5,000 and seizure of the aircraft are authorized penalties.

Low flying over swamps and marshes is tempting to some, especially if it is known that there is no natural feature of above, say, 300 feet in the area, but it is dangerous, and in 1972-73 there were 198 unwarranted low flying accidents with fatal outcomes in more than half.

Remember, too, the FAA Advisory Circular requesting pilots to maintain 2000 feet above protected areas and National Parks. This voluntary program is being monitored and if cooperation is inadequate, then "supplemental action" will be taken, whatever that means.

The only safe way to overfly swamp, marsh, bog, muskeg, savanna and wetland is to dogleg your route at altitude along railroads or highways or skirt the area entirely. This latter will be difficult as there are 74,000,000 such acres in U.S.A. You could, however, make a point of not visiting the States that are generously endowed with such "trembling earth," but this seems like cutting off your nose . . . As a matter of interest,

Desert, ocean or swamp—it's all the same to 55 Mike. She flies on just hoping that she's strapped to a pilot who knows his heading, his winds aloft and where he's at. Photo Credit: Margaret Anderson

File a flight plan when flying over any wet lands and up-date it constantly.

Florida has 17 million acres of swampland; Louisiana, Georgia and North Carolina share 20 million acres and among the Northern states, Minnesota leads with 5 million acres. Even in the dry far west, Arizona has 30,000 acres. That is a lot of real estate to try to avoid.

Don't ever expect to find lakes or waterbeds on the map agreeing with the ground or being easy to identify. To me, Minnesota was a series of circular lakes joined together like the Olympic symbol and all defying identification and Florida wet land seemed an unending, overgrown, stunted pasture with no features; even the tidal basins of Maryland maintained their anonymity despite the occasional landmark.

Fortunately for the pilot, the recognizable sea coastline is usually not more than one or two hours from America's major swamps and with brackets like that along your route, the destination should be ultimately found. If your journey becomes too tedious for your passengers, you may have to splice the main brace with your crew (but not the captain) since as far back as 200 years ago, swamp surveyor William Byrd said, "never was Rum, that cordial of life, found more necessary than in this Dirty Place."

Report your position at intervals and file a flight plan.

EMERGENCY LANDINGS ON WET LANDS are less easy than they look. Alaskan tundra, the summer bog created because the permafrost does not allow water drainage from the thaw, typifies the problem. The terrain looks inviting and level but is treacherously soft and like a landing in soft snow, the aircraft almost always goes over on its back. Even the most careful of soft field techniques with the wheel well back is usually inadequate in any wet land, and salt marsh grass is notorious for concealing rocks, roots, ruts and wretched rotten obstacles below its apparent smoothness.

The FAA booklet *Terrain Flying* advises Southern pilots setting down in

Tundra or bog looks deceptively smooth and an ideal landing surface but be forewarned.
Photo Credit: Alaskan Travel Division Dept. of Economic Development and Planning

Florida swamps to go for the areas between the pine and the cypress as the firmest, driest possibilities around. It is the overflow area for the swamp and usually devoid of trees. Usually bogs have stunted growth, and black spruce, for example, may attain a ground level diameter of only one inch in 30 years (I wonder if that is what's wrong with my blasted garden).

Assuming that you've by necessity dropped in to say "Howdy" to 400 kinds of insects and 700 species of fish, and that by luck you were wearing a tight shoulder harness, a yellow hard hat, had two ELT's and had filed a flight plan, what should you now do?

Well, the plane may have partly disappeared into the muck, and you are probably not too conspicuous, cheerful or comfortable. To quote Theodore Roethke, "as if I had broken the natural order of things in that swampland . . . as if I had committed, against the whole scheme of life, a desecration."

Game wardens say if you are lost in a swamp, sit down, light a fire and await rescue — don't wander. Lighting a fire may be difficult but you can build a platform with sticks above the water level and cover it with mud, then light your fire on top. Make sound signals, three shots or three whistle blasts. One hunter lost in the 1,000,000 acre Great Dismal Swamp between Virginia and North Carolina led rescuers to his position by blowing like a horn across the muzzle of his gun. He was lucky that his relief group had sharp eyes in that swamp as the cypress, swamp maple and pricky ash form such a dense canopy in places that the fish are blind in the perpetual darkness of some areas.

I can't tell you what to do if an alligator attacks you — I don't even remember the difference between a crocodile and an alligator (or a camel and a dromedary either for that matter). However, insects, leeches, a few water snakes and immersion foot are more likely problems. Leeches usually can be brushed off easily

117

and if not, a pinch of salt may kill them. A hot ember or a cigarette end makes them back off. You should then apply a tight bandage to the wound as it will tend to bleed freely. Loathsome things, leeches — as an M.D. I much prefer the insult "quack" to the word "leech." Immersion foot or trench foot is hard to prevent if you are up to your knees in what Nicholas Harman calls "a tangle of mucky roots and wriggling watery life." Try to keep your feet dry, wiggle your toes, and change your socks if possible. Remove your footwear as often as you can to allow

judge its safety from its color. Often peat has filtered the water and made it safe. Leaves and vegetation may stain the water which may, nevertheless, be okay to drink. Black and sweet gum and cypress stain the water dark, and juniper and cedar stain it yellow. In Wisconsin, I noticed the water was stained dark due to tannic acid from tree roots. I found that the Indians used the water as an antiseptic for burns, and in fact, in World War II, tannic acid was a favorite dressing for burned servicemen (which is the origin of the tea bag first aid treatment for kitchen

Treat any wetlands cross country like an overwater flight; know your fuel consumption and your point of no return.   *Photo Credit: Florida News Bureau Dept. of Commerce*

your feet to breathe. You can sling your wet socks round your neck or from your belt to dry and change them every hour or so. If you have a fire going, you can heat sand in a can, then pour it into your boots to dry them. As Charles Jansen says, "Happiness is fresh clean socks and mosquito netting."

Water is not a problem; but you cannot

burns). You can filter water yourself through charcoal or attempt the Boy Scout method for purifying water, which is: remove your long pants and turn one leg inside out inside the other, knot the bottom with a shoe lace, support on a tripod of sticks, fill with water and drop in very hot stones until the water is boiling, then keep going a little bit longer.

Cool and drink.

O.K. You are crouched on a slight elevation, with a fire going and a water supply. Food comes next and shouldn't be too much of a problem with the fish and bird life around. You may be able to set fish traps if the marsh is tidal, or you can fasten baited hooks to floating sticks and simply keep checking to see if you have been lucky. Birds can be caught by a cruel method, which may be justified in survival situations, by soaking any grain, pea or bean to soften it, then inserting a wire through-and-through so that about one-eighth of an inch protrudes outside. This bait is snapped up by the bird, and the wire punctures his crop to kill him. Alternately, you can look for bird droppings to locate bird areas, then fasten to a floating log a fishhook baited with, for example, a dead frog. The bird will then get caught just like a fish. An alternative way which is more complicated is to fasten a line to a balanced rock which, disturbed by the bird's antics, falls off the log, pulling the bird to the bottom to drown it.

FIRE

SWAMP FIRE on platform of logs

SWAMP SURVIVAL

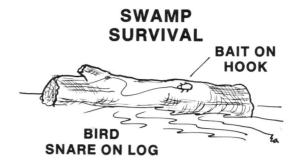

BAIT ON HOOK

BIRD SNARE ON LOG

You can test an area with different baits as a trial to see which is preferred.

Amongst plant life, cattails are edible. The root stalk is 46% starch and 11% sugar, and even the growing stalks and pollen can be eaten. What was that? Sorry, I don't have a recipe for gatorburgers.

If you decide to strike out for civilization, you must have a compass as wandering in a circle is a real hazard. If you are following the sun as a direction, remember the sun moves. Many tired, exhausted, lost souls have stumbled in a half circle forgetting as they referred to the sun that it circled also.

If the sky is overcast and the sun cannot be located, rub your fingernail on your forehead sweat to make it greasy, then stand a small twig upright on it. A faint shadow should show up to demonstrate the sun's direction.

As you travel, watch your footing. Your shoes are probably vital to your ability to cover terrain and they can easily be sucked off in the muck of the swamp. Quicksand may be a real hazard, and the writer Max Gunther saw two of his friends die in the Everglades quicksand. Gerard Matthes of the United States Geological Survey advises from personal experience if caught in quicksand not to panic or you are lost. He once took ten hours to escape from a quicksand when he fell into a bog while working by himself. General rules are, if you are just starting to sink step back; if knee deep, freeze and remove your pack; if going down fast, try to roll over onto your back and spread your arms out into a cross. Make slow deliberate

SUN DIRECTION
WHEN SKY
OVERCAST

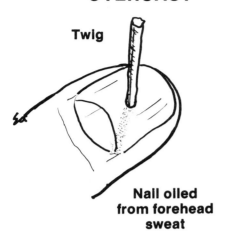

Twig

**Nail olled
from forehead
sweat**

moves. You may manage a shallow breast stroke on your face, but whatever you do, don't wave your arms in the air. Quicksand is impressive. In the late 19th century, a Kansas Pacific Railroad engine disappeared into one in the Kiowa Creek, Colorado washout; the Allied Armies lost vehicles in Germany towards the end of World War II and even now, bulldozers and their crews still occasionally disappear forever at construction sites.

If attempting to cross a river, attempt to cut yourself a tall staff, then angle down and across the current. If wearing a pack, undo the waist belt of the pack in case you get pulled under. You can float your pack over by wrapping it in a waterproof sheet and swimming with it, but pack the bottom of the poncho package with loose grass or brush to absorb any leakage of water. Under certain circumstances, a rope may be tied to the middle of a stick which is then flung across to catch in trees or rock. The rope should then be tightened above water level and you should cross by moving your feet sideways, as you face upstream on the downstream side of the rope.

Survival near seashores may be relatively easy. Fish is a-plenty, and there will be driftwood for fires. The breeze will keep away insects, and there will be no mud, just sand that dries quickly. It can be miserably hot without shade, but shelters of rock are easily constructed. But remember to do so above the high water mark. If you move from the location, stay close to the sea and work your way along the shoreline, not inland. Look at that! You're rescued already; here comes a beautiful blonde in a bikini to save you.

Photo Credit/opposite page: U.S. Dept. of Agriculture, Forest Service

9
FLYING
FORESTS

"The American forest, our last national frontier,
appears endless and abundant. That's the illusion"
JACK SHEPHERD

FORESTS

Below your wing, a green carpet stretching to all quadrants of the compass, teeming with life and interesting phenomena and looking for all the world as if *any* pilot could land like thistledown his frail craft on the moss-like tops of trees.

T'ain't so, and forests are to be avoided like any other example of wilderness terrain. How do you avoid something which is so plentiful? About 33% of the world land mass is forested; in comparison, 39% of North America's land mass is wooded. North America has about 23% of all the forests in the world, which contrasts with Europe's 3%.

Forests grow where they are assured a summer temperature of at least 50 degrees F (how come they grow in Maine, then? Hush.) and an annual rainfall of 16-20 inches. They are a great help to Mother Nature by reducing wind movement, moderating air temperatures and balancing evaporation and humidity. They are no great help to pilots and swallow aircraft with certain regularity. When planes vanish over forests, they really disappear and often a hunter in the Fall will stumble onto a wreck that has been lost for many years.

Rules are similar to flying swamps or over water but in practice we are surrounded so by forests that it becomes impractical always to be dog legging. The true utility of the aircraft is lost if we can't fly direct and there are many times when the only sensible way to fly over forested terrain is to choose and preflight carefully a good plane, verify adequate gas and good weather, file a flight plan, hold a heading and fly.

In cruise, confirm wind direction and note every and any open space of field as you pass by as you may wish to return to it. Monitor the gauges and stay in radio communication. Be prepared for turbulence on landing roll as hedgerows and trees often cause abberations in air flow to catch the unwary. As always, carry a survival kit including a good knife, matches and insect repellent. Pilots have found the loneliness of flying over the North American forest striking; but, of course, in the Fall, the foliage alone justifies the journey.

Emergency landings in trees are a technique all their own. Continue to fly the aircraft with full flaps at minimum controllable speed directly into the wind. Don't stall and drop it in. Continue to fly with control to the end. Don't line up with one tree but go between once you are on the ground. The National Transportation Safety Board report NTSB-AAS-72-3 gives us this cute advice about landing in trees: "aim for the softest," but, in fact, it is a most interesting document. David Leach, naturalist, says, "trees loom large . . . in the prosaism of our everyday lives" and you'll notice that for sure on your emergency approach.

If the aircraft stays stuck in the upper branches, take care making your exit. If it seems secure, drop or lower as much gear from it as seems practical. Fasten a rope to it and the trees and climb down as best you can. The ideal is to have a secure rope attached to the *tree* for climbing down; but on the ground a line attached to the *plane* that you can pull on, in the hope of bringing the aircraft to ground level for survival purposes.

Stranded in a huge, vast forest you are probably better off than in any other survival location. A knife is vital and, of course, to the American Indian, was the most essential of any items available. With a substantial knife, shelters can be constructed of saplings and spruce, beds can be woven, fire can be struck and food killed. Shelter will be necessary as our woods are usually humid with rainfalls of 50 inches. The insect plague is the greatest misery of all the forest life that touches stranded man and in the absence of net and repellents, try to use long sleeved, long legged clothing. Oil can be attempted on the skin as a repellent but mud is probably better. Nothing will be completely satisfactory and survivors rescued from the woods are usually a dreadful sight from insect bites. Avoid damp locations, and try to build your shelter where there is the touch of a breeze.

You are surrounded by plenty from larvae and grubs to grasshoppers. A useful book is Bradford Angier's *How to Survive In The Woods* (c) Collier Books, New York. You may be lucky enough to be competing with squirrels for nuts like beech nuts, pecans, walnuts, chestnuts, hazel nuts and butternuts and even acorns are edible if you boil to remove the bitterness and throw away the water. The Indians added hardwood ash to the water to absorb the bitterness.

Fire is the difference between rescue and defeat. In Winter, a fire will attract less attention but three fires are a sign of distress. During the summer season, fire lookout towers and aircraft surveillance patrols will have a fire noted very quickly. Black smoke caused by oil or rubber added to the fire makes it more significant. A tree standing out in the open can be prepared as a torch tree, to be ignited if any aircraft passes over. Be circumspect about your use of fire as in the ten years 1950-1960, 1,435,000 fires were recorded in the United States, or about 400 a day. Each year 21,650,000 acres (or an area the size of the State of Maine) are damaged by fire to a loss of $500 million a year. Bush pilots often tease fire spotters and say, "If I come down, you'll find me on the upwind side of the biggest fire you've ever seen!"

Minimal forest survival kit includes mosquito netting, insect repellent, matches, a compass and a sensible knife.   *Photo Credit: E. G. Anderson*

Unless you are a seasoned, experienced outdoorsman, you are much better to stay put and hope for rescue after fire signaling than to strike out for civilization. If moving, use a compass and blaze the trees so you can find your way back if necessary. Remember, should you stumble into any wild animal. he is going to be more frightened than you, even though he isn't lost.

Be comforted by Harry Roberts, "We don't go into the woods to rough it, we go to smooth it. We get it rough enough at home."

In flying over any remote forest, look for signs of man and head for them if you have engine trouble.
Photo Credit: Oregon State Highway Travel Section

"Since before the dawn of history Man has been a voyager.
Some men have sunk and some have burned and
some have won home to end their days on the beach
dreaming of the other days."
FOLKLORE AND THE SEA
Horace Beck
(c) 1973 Mystic Seaport, Inc.
Mystic Seaport, Connecticut

10
OVERWATER
FLYING

OVER WATER FLYING

The enormity of the ocean and man's puny insignificance over it and worse, in it, is soon apparent to any pilot or passenger who departs from sheltered shores. You promise your crew an island vacation marvel — take care lest you "write promises in water." If I were an innocent passenger in an aircraft challenging terrain, I suspect I would wish certain characteristics in my pilot. For flying the desert, I'd trust that he knew his map readings; for the mountains, I'd want him to have the common sense to ask local pilots for advice if in doubt; for frozen wastes, I'd require him to have the wisdom of knowing when the weather was telling him it's a no-go; and for over water flying, he would have to know the numbers for his plane — he'd have to be able to do the mathematics, the calculations, the pencil sucking, ear scratching figuring of plane against time against weather.

It is in over water flying that I see my wife at her reluctant hero worst. This is when her phrases flow: I am her "flying fool" or the "incompleat pilot," our plane "the flying coffin" and she'll quote me Thomas Fuller, "The fool wanders, the wise man travels." When Women's Lib became strong, I received my new pilot's license and, teasing her, pointed out that it called me not an airperson but an airman. Her sardonic reply: "You're lucky that's all it calls you." However, despite Adlai Stevenson's comment that "no craft, no crew can travel safely with such vast contradictions," she has tolerated her ultimate in family flying — going over water ("I can't swim") and flying at altitude ("Isn't it safer lower down, dear?") She has accepted fog in Long Island Sound, haze over Nantucket, an oil leak over the Bahamas and flew with me among the Outer Hawaiian Islands

when the radio was abuzz with the search for a crashed Bonanza.

Let us look at the requirements for over water flying.

The Pilot: Can he swim, does he have any knowledge of the sea, any lore of the ocean? Has he seen enough high seas from a deep sea fishing vessel to respect maritime weather? Arthur Beiser talking of a gale says, "A poor word to describe the screaming wind that inflames the sea into cusps of white-flecked malevolent fury." Charlton Ogburn, Jr. also knew the sea as "roiled and tormented . . . a riot of leaping waves and frothing whitecaps." And that, my friend, is what you might have to ditch into. Are you comfortable flying at altitude, are your passengers ill-at-ease or scared by emptiness? If so, reassure them and even, although it might seem to have the opposite effect, go through a brief ditching rehearsal. Think of their comforts. Are they warm enough? For a long flight, do you have drinks and snacks? And especially important, do you have a receptacle with a lid, for the bladder sitting on each seat? Do they have magazines or books to read? Are clothes suitable? A cap with a visor for any front seat passenger will be appreciated if you are flying into the sun.

How are you on an important pilot skill; namely, slow flight on the backside of the power curve? Since this is a significant part of ditching procedure, you should practice it at altitude including with full flaps.

The Plane: Is it absolutely in the best of shape? If you are taking it out of the country, are all the papers in order and is your insurance valid? In some countries, listing one of your passengers as co-pilot saves expense. Do you know the regulations FAR 91.189 for overwater survival gear and FAR 99 for ADIZ regulations? The Canadian government has thorough and helpful rules for aircraft leaving its shores, just as its cold weather survival kits are a model to follow.

Verify that you have the necessary flotation gear on board and an ELT that will float. You must have trustworthy radio navigation equipment as lives will depend on it. Test it by VOT or other method, prove it is accurate, then trust it. An auto pilot is a godsend for long tiring trips.

Be familiar with AIM data, current Notams, radio stations and have up-to-date maps. Carry sturdy tiedowns, control locks and wheel chocks. If you are

The Coast Guard overwater vest can be copied by any civilian for only a few dollars, then packed with the items the professionals feel are the necessities. Clockwise bottom: floating bladders, sea dye markers, whistle, strobe, mirror, flares and gun, smoke signals, personal radio set. *Photo Credit: E. G. Anderson*

A further look at the contents of the Coast Guard vest. Clockwise bottom right: signaling mirror, personal radio, strobe, whistle, sea dye marker, smoke signal, flares and gun.
Photo Credit: E. G. Anderson

How far can you really get from 10,000 feet at best glide speed with power off? Know the maximum time aloft and maximum distance speed. In short be completely familiar with the airplane to which you are entrusting your family, and comfortable with the mathematics involved in dead reckoning and navigation. George Kunzie before his first North Atlantic crossing in a light plane, said, "The E 6 B computer becomes your best friend." Know your point of no return.

Preflight is preceded by the most meticulous fastidious weather briefing you've ever had. How many hours of daylight? What's the synoptic weather picture — where are the fronts — where are the icing levels — winds aloft? What's happening out to sea; haze, fog, clouds, storms, and what are the emergency and rescue procedures and frequencies? What are airline frequencies in that geographical area? The U.S. Coast Guard lists sea conditions and wind as the most important factors in ditching with type of aircraft and pilot skill following in less importance. Don't fly in marginal VFR

renting, the choice should be low wing retractables as a NASA (NACA in the old days) trial 10 years after World War II indicated how much better they do in ditching than fixed gear high wing planes. When wheels catch water surfaces, any aircraft tends to go over on its back, and low wing aircraft do not submerge their cabins as quickly as high wing planes. On the other hand, high wing aircraft are less likely to damage flaps or ailerons during preliminary impact with better control and less likely to lose a wing with loss of flotation. The NASA study done at Langley Field in Virginia also showed that larger aircraft ditch better than small ones.

Whichever plane you have, you must know the numbers for it. Know its oil consumption and fuel flow. Learn by your own experience how accurate the fuel gauges are by running a tank dry at different power settings. Test glide distances at altitude at different glide speeds.

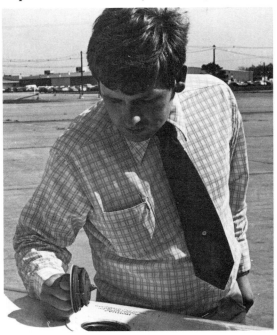

If you were limited to only one preflight action, you'd check your fuel on board. Yet fuel mismanagement is the commonest cause of ditching and it can happen to you.
Photo Credit: Gillian Anderson

weather as haze and fog can both contribute to loss of horizon and make you IFR before you know it.

Know the Beaufort scale for wind at sea:

Wind
Velocity
(Knots)   Sea Indications

Calm	Glassy — like a mirror.
1-3	Ripples with appearance of scales.
4-6	Small wavelets. Crests have glassy appearance but do not break.
7-10	Large wavelets with some crests beginning to break.
11-16	Small waves with frequent whitecaps.
17-21	Moderate waves, foam and many whitecaps.
22-27	Large waves begin to form. Extensive foam with some spray.
28-33	Sea heaps up foam in streaks blown in direction of waves.
34-40	Moderately high waves. Well marked foam streaks.
41-47	High waves with spray affecting visiblity.
48-54	Very high waves with overhanging crests. Visibility affected.

Or to summarize, the *absence* of whitecaps indicates a wind of less than 10 knots. The *presence* of many whitecaps indicates a wind of 10-20 knots, and seas of usually three to four feet. Whitecaps with many streaks of foam behind them indicate winds of 20-30 knots and seas of four to six feet. Blowing spray indicates winds in excess of 30 knots and seas greater than seven feet (after AOPA).

In cruise, note the position of any vessel you pass and survey the ocean swell below you. You cannot really read the swell pattern below 1500 feet but it can be readily understood at 2500 feet. Calculate and remember your ditching heading; you can request of the Coast Guard best headings for forced landings on water and they will compute it for current conditions in your area. Keep in radio contact and be wary if you realize after fifteen minutes that you've not heard activity on your radio as this may indicate that you've lost your frequency. As you know, HF radio is required over the open

You have previously weighed your baggage carefully, prepared a little card with ditching checklist information on it, filed a flight plan and checked your oil level and topped your tanks. No pilot should ever fly away from land without maximum fuel as fuel exhaustion is the commonest cause of ditching (in a large series of cases, only one ditching in five was due to engine failure). Better to leave behind one of your suitcases than not be able to fill up with fuel. There are all sorts of horror stories about fuel mismanagement and subsequent ditching — in fact, in New England alone in 1972 there were seventeen general aviation accidents involving unscheduled water landings with eleven fatalities.

With coral and gravel runways so common, any rented plane should have its tires and propeller carefully inspected for any defect. Life jackets should be worn uninflated and shoulder harnesses attached to seat belts.

On takeoff, adjust your DG to the runway heading, turn to the heading you want and recheck any ADF or VOR. Fly your VOR radial checking it against magnetic compass and DG until you get the flag, then maintain your heading from your magnetic compass, changing your DG as it precesses. Stay overland as much as you can if practical. Request radio or radar surveillance, and report often to give your position. Cross check by radio fix if possible.

sea as VHF communication is unreliable because of the distances involved, and other factors.

Attempt en route to get a fix to confirm winds aloft but be sure to identify your radio navigation frequency as, on occasion, bizarre freak situations will allow another far distance station with the same frequency to jump across the ocean.

If you have to ditch, try to do so in shallow water and know your ditch heading at all times.
Photo Credit: Piper Aircraft Corporation

In overwater flying, don't count on being able to land on any islands or rocks which your maps demonstrate.
Photo Credit: Nova Scotia Information Centre

Calculate your gas situation as you approach your point of no return, and stay at altitude to confirm destination weather before let down.

Clouds build up over land to facilitate island detection which is fine in the Hawaiian Islands where the distant volcanoes peep through the clouds to resemble the bald dome of a monk with a curly fringe. In flat coral islands, however, you cannot be sure that land lies under yonder distant cloud and many errors have been made by pilots who lose their heading and wheel off to investigate for landing.

Use your check list for landing as you may have been in cruise for so long that your brain may have packed in for the day. Don't expect an island tower operator to have radar or to be able to see

Usually ditching close to land makes sense, but the seashore can be less hospitable than the shallow edge of a lake. Height over water is, however, easier to judge if land reference is also present.

Photo Credit: E. G. Anderson

With beach landings, go for the sand that is still damp as it has been packed solid by wave action.
Photo Credit: Alaska Travel Division, Dept. of Economic Development and Planning

you against the ocean, so give him plenty of help when you call in for landing. More primitive strips should be overflown above traffic pattern then dragged as you would any rough field. This will also alert any resort operator that a plane is landing. Even if the field is unattended, announce your intentions on 122.8 in the blind, and watch out for other traffic since your isolation for the over water trip may have made you careless in that respect. Use a soft field technique and watch for crazy winds, thermals and turbulence as you come in for hot land after the smooth ocean ride. Watch out for nosewheel or prop damage if the surface is rough, taxi carefully and secure the aircraft well as some islands have brisk wind (like hurricanes, maybe). Supervise the refueling yourself.

Beach landings on sand may offer themselves through choice or necessity. Sounds great! No approach obstacles, smooth surfaces, long runway with plenty of overrun. However, any pilot who has spent part of his day hosing down with fresh water sea planes used in salt water may wonder if it is worth the trouble and risk.

If you know a delightful cove with a satisfactory beach, be aware that the sea constantly changes the land and a suitable spot in 1978 may be gone a few years hence. Some beaches are too soft or too rocky, or may be broken up by streams or currents. Know the State and National Park regulations about landing on beaches.

The best time to land is with an ebbing tide which leaves you wet packed sand and some hours before your plane is awash with the return of the tide. High tide landings leave only a portion of unsuitable soft land for landing and should

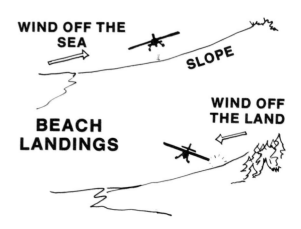

WIND OFF THE SEA

SLOPE

BEACH LANDINGS

WIND OFF THE LAND

be avoided. The sand is also too soft on the land side of any inlet as it has not been packed by wave action.

Drag the surface first, being prepared for bubbling turbulence over sand dunes or cliffs. Depth perception may be poor as in a bright sun there is almost a glassy water whiteout phenomenon.

Touch down holding a tad of power with the nose slightly up and feel and assess the surface with your main wheels before you cut power.

Wind assessment prior to touchdown is important. You will almost always be landing parallel to the water's edge and the wind will be cross wind off the sea or off the land. If the wind is off the water, your upwind wing will be down and your plane's lateral axis will parallel the slope of the beach. However, a wind from the land if more than 20 knots may have you dropping your upwind wing to control and digging into the sand.

DITCHING

As John Vandegrift says, "All overwater flights end up one of two ways; wet or dry," and even Shakespeare reminds us, "There is a tide in the affairs of man."

The biggest problem with ditching is the refusal of the pilot to believe that the need has happened to him. The Hawaiian Islands have a survival rate of about 80% for their ditchings; warm water, prompt dispatch of rescue vessels, flight following radio contact and pilot awareness and training have all contributed to this high figure. If you are completely lost on the open sea with low fuel, accept the need to ditch early and get your procedures set up.

Get high for better visibility — maybe you'll see a boat or an island, and for better radio navigation help or voice contact. Get out your Mayday with particular reference to your position and intentions. Broadcast in the blind if there is

Watch for turbulence and wind shear over any coastline, here the North Shore of Molokai, Hawaiian Islands.
Photo Credit: Margaret Anderson

In any beach area, the coastal highway may be your only possible emergency landing site.

Photo Credit: Oregon State Highway Department

no reply and squawk 7700 on the transponder. IF you get contact, you should state the nature of the problem, your heading, speed and altitude, and the type of help you require. Conserve your fuel supply as a Coast Guard intercept may be possible. So get high, get out your Mayday and get out your Flight Manual and your ditching card check list. Turn your heading bug to your ditch heading.

If you're going down, you are going to lose your aircraft and belongings and perhaps your life so this is no time to hold on to sentimental or expensive possessions. Dump belongings out to lighten the aircraft unless they will have subsequent value in the open sea. Stow gear as, shortly, you are going to be rattled like dice. Secure your life jacket but do not inflate it yet. Get the back of your

DITCHING
HIGH WINDS

WIND ⟶

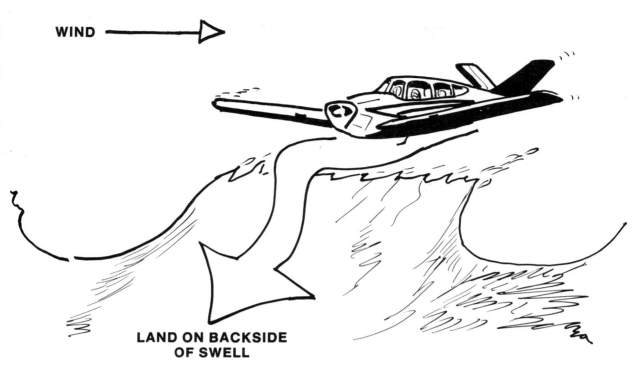

LAND ON BACKSIDE OF SWELL

seat upright and tighten your shoulder harness and seat belts. Get a jacket jammed at the door hinge and a garment or cushion for each passenger's face. Have the survival gear and raft handy and a flashlight exactly where you will be able to find it. Empty pockets of sharp objects, remove pens, false teeth and glasses.

If you haven't been able to work out a ditching heading, you can fly low over the sea on different headings until you spot one that seems to be suitable. You have below you the longest runway in the world and if you still have power, you can take time to do it right. Dark compounds the problem and if you have enough fuel to last till dawn, defer till first light. On the other hand, if darkness is about to fall, perhaps you should ditch now as long as it is still light. If you are unfortunate enough to be ditching at night, leave lights on in the cabin to facilitate ease of

DITCHING
LOW WINDS

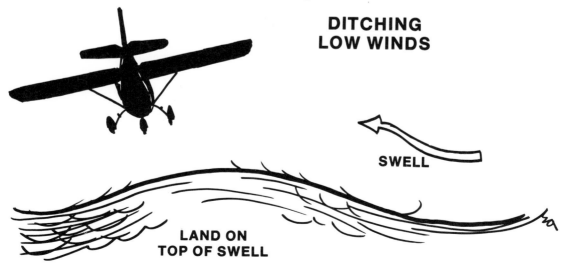

SWELL

LAND ON TOP OF SWELL

exit but do not use landing lights as the glare from the ocean surface will dazzle you.

Put on your flaps early and high to get the hang of feeling for the surface. You should be in slow flight with gear retracted in a slightly nose high attitude. Don't be too high with your nose or you will catch your tail, and slap in your nose and submarine. You'll need more power as you are behind the power curve. If you have no power, you should carry a faster approach speed. The flare can then be started earlier and more gradually as you feel for the landing. I found this technique in sea plane training gave me the only consistently good landings I've ever had in aviation, as if I was constantly moving the numbers of the threshold ahead of me to prevent an overshoot. On land, it only works if the runway length is unlimited.

You will be landing parallel to the swells with winds less than 25 knots and into the wind and into the swell movement for winds above 35 knots. For winds between 25 and 35 knots, you do a bit of both.

For 25 knots or less cross winds, the wind has to be ignored; the sideways drift is not critical as you are not on a narrow runway. Try to land on top of a swell, keeping your wings level by reference to the horizon initially then by reference to the swell tilt at the end. As you flare over the waves, shout to your passengers to hold on until the plane has stopped, then flying to the end, put the plane down in any suddenly appearing flat spot on the top of the swell.

For winds more than 35 knots, your "ground" speed will be so reduced in slow flight that you should land into the wind on the back side of a crest. Incidentally, for landing in a river, always land into the wind and ignore current direction.

Expect violent control stick movements as control surfaces slap the surface; be ready to let the control wheel go.

You can expect complete chaos next with all sorts of blurred visual impressions. Hold on until it is obvious the plane has stopped as it will often ricochet or skip across the surface before it digs in.

If you are ditching, communicate, climbing for reception if necessary. The Coast Guards are as close as your radio but give them some assistance before you go down.   *Photo Credit: E. G. Anderson*

You're down.

Your success at this point depends on the weather, the roughness of the sea, whether you are fortunate enough to be landing power-on low wing gear up or stuck with fixed gear high wing and a dead engine. Your success also depends on luck. If you catch a wingtip by not holding the wings level, you are probably going to cartwheel. When your fixed gear hits first, you are going to go over on your back, and forget about water in your bathtub being nice and soft — this stuff you are now into is like a brick wall. Hence, the first rule: Don't relax or let go after the first impact. Hold on, expect a second bang. Wait until the plane stops, then get out fast. How fast? Well, in Robert Trumbull's book *The Raft* (c) 1942 Holt, Rinehart & Winston, Inc., an incredible true tale of the 34 days of survival of three Navy pilots in a 40 pound, four foot by eight foot rubber raft, Chief Petty Officer Dixon states, "Suddenly there was no airplane. It was there, and then it was gone . . . like a magician's trick."

Low wing aircraft with empty gas tanks may float for an unpredictable time, but the engine is so heavy in the average light plane, the aircraft will nose down and disappear in minutes. If you have not succeeded in getting a door jammed open prior to ditching, you may have to wait until there is enough water inside the plane to equalize the outside water pressure and allow the door to swing open. Whether you have the front seat as far back as possible before impact to maximize ease of front seat exit, or far forward to allow rear seat passengers the best chance out will depend on many factors, including time. In theory, residual air in the cockpit will be under the roof at the rear as you nose down and fill with water but don't count on it. It may be so dark and confused in the cockpit that orientation can be difficult, but don't panic — if your preliminary check shows that you are still in your seat and your seat is still attached where it should be,

your direction of movement should be obvious. Don't inflate your life jacket until you are outside the aircraft, or you may get stuck in the exit. As you leave the aircraft, try to drag out behind you any objects which will float, unless so doing will impede the exit of others. Grab cushions, your empty two pound coffee can urinal, any sick bags, hats, bottles, women's purses or handbags, If your survival kit was where it should be — on top — that should be snatched up and any water container or camp gear which will hold air. Take a moment *now* to think. What do you have routinely in your aircraft that you would grab — and I don't mean Elke Sommer. Even a can of oil can be punctured, drained and used upside down for buoyancy. People have floated with the help of hats, inflated Saran Wrap bags, upside down pots and pans, empty aerosol cans, emptied wine bottles and even perfume bottles have helped augment swimmers' efforts.

Once you are outside the aircraft, try to keep a cool head. Your natural buoyancy will bring you up to the surface even if you can't swim. Try not to thrash around as you may injure others exiting. Anthony Greenbank says, "Make like a bottle not a battle" and you'll reach the surface. The human body will float fully clothed vertically if the lungs are inflated, with five pounds of body weight above the surface. Since the head weighs almost 15 pounds, this means that in almost 99% of males, the water line will be at the forehead. In women (who have more body fat), the water line will be at the nose, unless they have very fat thighs which tends to make their body float less vertically. This is the basis for the famous "drownproofing" method taught by Fred R. Lanoue of Atlanta, Georgia. This one man is credited with saving the lives of thousands of airmen in World War II when his methods were taught to Navy pilots in their basic training. Lanoue once drownproofed 1000 children under the age of five years to demonstrate how hard it is for a trained person to drown. The children in their test floated for one hour then swam a mile. They then had their ankles tied together and floated for one half hour, then swam another mile. They then swam another mile fully dressed with their wrists tied together!

You are now alive in a confusing mass of water. You have survived the first crisis in ditching; namely, the crash itself. The second crisis follows immediately after and involves getting your party together and on the raft. The third crisis is more languid and is the duress of man's survival afloat on the open sea.

Try to make a quick assessment of the situation at this stage. Where is the sun, the wind direction, what way is the current flowing? Where is the aircraft? What floating debris is close by, and most important of all, where are the others?

If you are a strong swimmer, don't undress yet. Survival on the raft may depend on clothing and contents of pockets. If the raft is right beside you, grab a rope and secure it to you while you find the others. A scissors kick will raise you high enough from the water for a better view. If there are peaks and troughs in the sea, use the opportunity when you are high on the sea to look around and search your horizon for others. It is probably better as others collect, to hang from the ropes around the raft until excitement and exhaustion are both relieved.

Be cautious about approaching a conscious drowning person or there will be two deaths instead of one. Try to reach over by extending an article of clothing like a shirt or towel, or a piece of debris or the tow bar. If you cannot reach, try to throw him a line, cushion, a half empty can, a thermos picnic cooler, even a cardboard box, or any floating material. If you swim over to help, try even in the confusion of the crash to recall principles of lifesaving. Don't swim head first to any conscious struggling person. Come up from behind, do a quick reversal by putting your legs between the person and yourself, then attempt the chin pull whereby if you are right handed, you reach over the victim's left shoulder and grab his chin with your left hand. Treading water to keep afloat and still holding the chin, you now reach over his right shoulder tucking it into your right armpit with your right hand under his left arm. He is now locked into the cross chest carry and your left arm is now free for the arm stroke.

This basic rescue technique is tiring and requires practice. If you are not in good training or physical shape, you will not be able to maintain this effort and you should regard this assist as a temporary expedient until you get the victim's Mae West inflated and him into the raft.

If the victim is conscious and struggling, he may have the strength of many men and you may have to defend yourself against his irrational attack. If he won't release his hold on you and you are yourself in peril, go underwater dragging him with you as this usually breaks a hold.

At this point, you are presumably glad that you can swim, but you know, Red Cross estimates that 40% of the U.S. population cannot swim twenty feet to safety and that is the range of one half of all drowning accidents. There are 6,000 to 8,000 drownings a year in the United States. Writer Jean Carper refers to a University of Georgia study of 1,309 drownings. 71% were nonswimmers, 22% were fair swimmers and only 1% of the deaths were in excellent swimmers. However, 200 people a year die in the United States trying to save others and lifeguards say that every sixth person they pull from the water is a would-be rescuer. To prevent what the Red Cross calls "the fatal rescue," remember their creed — row, throw, tow, go and go last. If you are attempting a rescue, constantly check your reference points by checking sun direction or the quadrant that clouds lie in and keep asking yourself: Where is the coastline? Where are the others? Where's the raft?.

Water skiers have drowned in cold

water with their lifejackets lying unused in the boat. That is why it makes sense to fly over water with your Mae West worn although not inflated. The greatest catastrophe in a ditching would be for the plane to sink with the raft still inside. The raft is the difference between life and death although there are anecdotes in plenty to belie that. A woman once floated for 37 hours off the coast of New Jersey until rescued with only a two inch slab of buoyant cushion for help. Way back in August 1969, a Korean, Chung Nam Kim, fell overboard without a life jacket one hundred miles offshore. When rescued by the Swedish ship Citadel, he had spent the last three hours of his despair riding on the back of a turtle.

Next in importance after raft is lifejacket. The U.S. Coast Guard tells of Captain Shook who ejected 60 miles off Florida and was rescued in shark infested waters after 39 hours in a lifejacket. On another occasion, a U.S. Navy Pilot swam for 73 hours in a lifejacket before reaching shore. After the Battle of Midway, six Japanese sailors survived 5½ days in lifejackets.

Perhaps the most incredible tale of sea survival without lifejackets is the story of the four Hawaiian fishermen who were five miles off the shore of Molokai in 1939 when their vessel sank. They realized that the side currents would carry them out to sea if they struck out for the shore, and confidently decided to swim to Oahu 20 miles distant. For 14 hours, they swam breaststroke while chatting and talking amongst themselves in a relaxed, almost blase fashion. They came ashore near Diamond Head, by chance walking past a reporter from a Honolulu paper. They were unimpressed by their own efforts and quite surprised by their subsequent press reception.

Of course, the important factor is water temperature. Of the 641 American airmen downed in the Arctic in World War II, few survived. In water less than 41 degrees F, few will live beyond half an hour, and unless you are very young and

fit, 30 degrees F kills in five minutes. The case of U.S. sailor William Peters is unique — he survived and was rescued after thirty minutes floating amongst ice floes. In the Titanic disaster, the water was 28 degrees F and half of the 1500 persons who drowned died of cold in the first half hour.

A 22-year-old pilot survived two hours of swimming in water 45-50 degrees F when his plane crashed one April off the coast of Oregon; five of his crew perished in the cold water and when he was rescued, initially, no pulse could be detected.

Cold water has no friends and defies even trained swimmers. The North Channel of the Irish Sea usually has temperatures of 49-53 degrees F and was unconquered until Tom Blower, age 33 and weighing 250 pounds, crossed its 22 miles in 1947. The famous swimmer, Jason Zirganos, a major in the Greek army, attempted to add this stretch of cold water to his many records in September 1959 but died at the age of 46 when he was hauled unconscious after 16½ hours only three miles off the coast of Scotland. A doctor in the boat opened his chest with a penknife to massage his heart but the patient died of ventricular fibrillation due to the cold. Most distance swimmers cultivate obesity but fat apparently is of little insulation help below 55 degrees F.

Cord Troebst, in his book *The Art of Survival* (c) 1965 Doubleday, describes an experiment where a volunteer, naked, collapsed after only 90 seconds at −211 degrees F (frankly, I'm surprised that he lasted that long), whereas the same man wearing special clothing tolerated to −418 degrees F the same time.

Nevertheless, the overall figures from World War II are encouraging: two-thirds of all Allied airmen adrift in warm water were saved and one-third of those in cold water. Cold water attacks your heart and respiratory muscles. I remember once falling through ice after a snowmobile accident. Since my children were watching, I resolved, in the split second that I fell through, to show them how a mature man behaves under stress. I intended to give them languid casual instructions about pushing branches toward me and to coordinate the rescue. Instead, I found myself unable to breathe and the choking, grunting shriek from my lips would have been more appropriate from a little girl!

If you intend to swim to shore, you should recall that the best you can do is two knots and since currents can exceed five knots, you will have to swim across them. George Llano has researched data of swims to survival and experimental swims. At a rate of 2.2 miles per hour, the crawl stroke burns 1600 calories of energy an hour; the breast stroke 1900 calories and the backstroke 2100 calories. A slower rate of 1 mile per hour lowers your energy requirements for crawl and breast stroke to 410 calories an hour. Remember, you are more interested in distance than speed. Intersperse simple floating for rest at intervals in your swimming attempt.

Drowning is usually due to panic and exhaustion. Fatigue is the enemy. Even "drownproofing" fails if the patient is unconscious, incapacitated by injury or pinned underwater. Anxiety causes hyperventilation with the chemical changes in the blood which can cause blackouts and subsequent drowning. In November 1802, the Dutch ship Vryheid sank in English waters with only 18 surviving of 472. An eyewitness saw a Captain of Marines swimming with one hand supporting his wife by the hair on her head. "Then came the moment when he was overcome by cold and fatigue. Turning around, he clasped her in his arms and both sank to their death in the sea." Edward Rowe Snow, *True Tales of Terrible Shipwrecks*, (c) 1963 Dodd, Mead & Company, New York.

The best life jackets are the yoke bib type which form a slab with a high collar on the neck. Even unconscious, you will be turned over to survive. The old cork life jackets were poor since they didn't keep the heads upright. In 1927, Germany

Your pants can be made into water wings to support any adult. Practice in your pool until the procedure is easy.
Photo Credit: E. G. Anderson

invented the inflatable life jacket and the same year, Admiral Byrd used a two man rubber dingy to good effect. In 1935 carbon dioxide inflation was developed, and when the U.S. Airship Macon crashed off the shore of California, 79 of 81 crew were saved by rubber rafts. However people learn slowly and in September 1955 when a DC 4 ditched in the open sea, the pilots couldn't relax for a moment of the 44 hours they were in the water because their Mae Wests were not designed to keep the heads upright free of the water.

If for some dumb reason you were flying over water without life jackets (and by the way if you were, you were dumb), you are now in the water temporizing until you can locate your raft (or did you forget your raft, too?). Despair not. Your clothes can be inflated. One pilot who regularly flies to the Bahamas is, to my knowledge, casual about life jackets but he keeps several Hefty Saran Wrap bags and a few elastic bands in the breast pocket of his shirt. These are his emergency inflation devices However, regular garments can be utilized as flotation assists also. Depending on water temperature and other needs, remove your shoes first, then socks, pants and shirt. You can inflate your pants by knotting the legs, closing the fly, then whipping them backwards and forwards in a V motion — not a circular motion — to fill them with air. The waistband should then be tied with a tie belt or shoe lace or simply closed shut and held folded over. You can also inflate the pants by blowing air into them underwater.

You can also inflate any button shirt you are wearing. Button the sleeves and the collar, tuck the tail into your belt, unbutton the third button down and huff and puff air into your shirt. The air will gradually be lost but can easily be replenished. Synthetic fabrics do not swell when wet and are not as air-tight as cotton and other natural fiber garments. You can also slap air into your open shirt front by cupping your hand and slapping water and air several times against your chest. You can also remove your shirt, knot the sleeves and put the shirt on backwards to inflate it as a collar around your neck. In 1962, an Alcatraz inmate swam three miles to freedom across the dreaded currents of San Francisco Bay by blowing air into his shirt. Underwater, your pants, shirt, underwear and socks weigh only one half pound so don't be in a great hurry to get rid of them.

A useful part of your sea survival kit is a simple whistle. The officers of the Titanic found this sound to travel well at sea and used it to rally people around them in the water.

You are now all hanging from the raft, collecting your second wind. You will find it less tiring if you face another person with the raft between you and hold each other's wrists. This is less exhausting than holding onto the float with fingerholds. Try to have a procedure for getting on to the raft. In fact, practice in a pool before your flight because it is not as easy as it looks and rafts frequently turn over with clumsy movements. If you have brought a victim to the raft, bring both his hands to the side of it. Then let him go, swim round to the other side, kick your legs, push with your arms and gain the deck. Support the victim's chin from the deck, then when you've rested (and, boy, will you be tired), kneel before the victim and drag him up and in by both arms.

Use the raft vigorously to search for any debris which later may be useful. Throw nothing away at this stage until, in collected fashion, you can analyze your future needs and whether the debris has any possible future value.

If by any odd quirk the plane is still afloat, you may consider entering it again to search for any useful items; but stay in the open door and be ready to vacate the plane promptly if it sinks. Any chart of the area will be useful and is probably well within reach. Try to break off the compass. Grab the tow bar and the control wheel lock; the ELT may be of the type that can be removed. Perhaps you could snatch the rear window blind or the string hammock that often lies unused in the baggage compartment. Even the IFR training hood may be of later value as a paddle or sunshield. Grab quickly, then get out because you have only moments before the plane sinks, and I suspect some readers would feel that it is folly to chance Fate by going back in.

You have now survived the drama of the crash, and the crisis of setting up your raft. You are ahead of the game and perhaps a bit lucky. Here now is where training and discipline pay off. In July 1816, the ship Medusa sank 100 miles from Africa. 150 crew and passengers scrambled in panic onto a large raft which had enough wine and water on board for their needs. Some, however, killed themselves, some drowned, some jumped overboard and all quarrelled. Within three days, there was murder and cannibalism and on the 12th day when they were rescued, only 15 were alive, of which 10 more died. More recently, in 1953 a 30-foot-long ferry ship "Mary Jeanne" from the Seychelles Islands went adrift. It rained 20 gallons which gave them a water supply. The survivors attempted to fish once and on failing, gave up and did not try again. As their comrades died, their bodies were flung overboard without any being kept as shark bait for fishing. All birds which came on board were eaten with nothing kept as fish bait. On the 74th day, the two survivors, aged 15 and 20, of the crew of 10 were rescued but they had not harvested the sea. In September 1962, a Superconstellation ditched 500 miles from Ireland with 78 passengers. There was only one 10-foot raft found, big enough for 25 people 48 people managed to fight their way on, the remainder perishing. Despite those tales of incompetence, there are, however, many splendid tales of how discipline and training and guts won the day.

Anthony Greenbank in his book *The Book of Survival,* (c) 1967 Harper and Row, states, "Even if you are paunchy, pregnant or generally past-it, survival advice presupposes that whoever faces catastrophe takes a deep breath and makes up his mind to have a really determined go at beating the odds."

What are the dangers you face now as you lie exhausted in your raft to endure your third crisis on the open sea? Perhaps thirst, hunger, loneliness, sea sickness, extremes of temperature and climate and sharks, although not necessarily in that order.

On the raft, your first priority is checking for injuries and taking inventory of possessions, assets and gear you have available. Throw nothing out yet as later, improvisation can make any odd item useful. For instance, when the English East Indian ship Fattysalam was wrecked in August 1761 on the Indian Seas, its longboat coasted to survival with its sail made from "ladies' petticoats and handkerchiefs." They were lucky — try nowadays making a sail out of jeans and Kleenex! Shoes can be used as paddles and as flotation buoys. The control wheel lock may be sharpened against another piece of metal and turned into a gaff for fishing. Don't throw away clothes or even rags as they will be used to catch fresh water in storms.

Artificial respiration is difficult, almost impossible, on a rubber raft but attempts may be indicated. The assessment of an injured person is covered in the chapter on Wilderness Medicine but mention should be made here of handling unconscious persons who have been submerged. Harvard University studies show that it takes three to five minutes to drown and that a person submerged one minute underwater has a 98% chance of survival; however, by a four minute submersion, the survival rate drops to 50%. Ten minutes submerged, there is only 1% chance and twelve minutes, the chance of survival is 0.1%. In their five year study of drowning, they did not find any case of survival if submerged for more than fifteen minutes.

However, in one Red Cross case,

Perhaps the most useful item in any survival kit and especially for pilots in the drink—the signaling mirror.
Photo Credit: E. G. Anderson

resuscitation was carried on for four hours with success ultimately. Start quickly even if the chance of survival is remote and keep it up until absolute exhaustion makes you quit or until rescue comes. Old methods of artificial respiration as taught in First Aid courses many years ago have now been replaced by cardiopulmonary resuscitation, CPR. Why not be trained by the American Heart Association in this skill? It's easy. There are hundreds of cases now on file where Boy Scouts, housewives and others who have attended simple instruction classes have brought back from the dead people too young or too well otherwise to die. It all seems so modern and new, yet the technique of the breath of life is mentioned in the Bible.

Perhaps the most dramatic incident involving the kiss of life was in 1962 when a 19-year-old youth in New Jersey was caught in a pool being emptied. He was dragged by the suction and held against the drain in nine feet of water. Fortunately, his predicament was spotted by two lifeguards who dove repeatedly to the

bottom to give mouth-to-mouth respirations for the eight minutes required before the valve could be turned off. The victim was then unconscious but recovered after five minutes of CPR.

Be prepared to signal early — the first plane overhead may be the only one — and in fact, your best chance of being picked up is in the first 12 hours. To look at statistics: few survive ten days at sea. Any plane flying higher than 1500 feet MSL is probably too high to spot a small raft, and it is pure chance if you are seen from a higher altitude. For this reason, as a general principle, rafts should be tied together to make a bigger air target. Swimmers in life jackets without rafts should link arms to support physically and emotionally the weaker swimmers, to defend against shark attack, and to make it easier for the party to be seen from the air.

One of my partners once lost his boat in Great Bay, New Hampshire and finally had to swim for one and a half miles against a diagonal current with three children. Although the boat remained vertically in the water. Directly under the downwind leg of a nearby Air Force Base, and other boats were sailing in the bay, no one noticed their predicament. Survival at sea is a bit like the lesson of life — you get out just about what you put in. Don't rely on others. "You have to work at survival."

Boats often pass castaways without seeing them, often as close as 250 yards. One survivor attracted a ship at night by striking his only match at the opportune time. John Fairfax, who rowed the 25 foot open boat Britannia across the Atlantic in 1969, comments on how often he was nearly run down at sea by larger ships whose officers of the watch were relying more on radar than vision. Castaway pilots Bertram and Klausman, adrift in the Timor Sea, fired four flares at a ship only 700 yards distant, but the ship passed on unknowing.

Okay, we've listed the dangers you face on your raft — the threats to your well being — so know your enemy. Reminds me of the Andy Capp cartoon where the football coach is shouting at his team as they run out to play, "Look at the other team! Know your enemy! They're the ones who have insulted your mother, made love to your wife, drunk your beer, stolen your property!", and Andy Capp calls to his coach, "Which is the one who drank my beer?"

Let us see what considerations we have.

THE RAFT

In World War II, one fifth of all Allied military aircraft forced landings had inadequate emergency equipment. Rescue attempts were poorly coordinated. Many of the rescue containers dropped by parachute were camouflaged and couldn't be located.

However, you are in a civilian situation. What you have is what you bought, or rented and checked before takeoff. Take care of the rubber. Avoid sharp objects and protect areas of wear. Keep touching it up with the repair kit and try to stay ahead of trauma to it by anticipating problems and safeguarding the raft. Rehearse methods of righting it if it overturns. The best way is for all to be on one side in the water, to reach over and pull on ropes attached to the other side when it will flip back quite easily, especially if you use wind direction to help. Expect the raft to turn over with sudden weather changes or wind shifts. Pilots Dixon, Pastula and Aldrich in their 34 day Pacific drift had numerous problems with their raft overturning. Have ropes attached streaming out behind the raft to grab if you fall overboard since an inflated raft with a stiff wind will skim "on the step" and leave you behind. Thor Heyerdahl almost lost some of the crew of his raft Kon Tiki when they found themselves in the water being speedily left behind by a fast moving raft. On a different ocean, another castaway fell to certain death from his raft which did not have a rope behind; however, a trailing fishing line caught its hook on his clothes such that he was able to pull the raft back to him for his ultimate survival.

When Dougal Robertson, the Scottish sailor-farmer was shipwrecked in 1972 by the attacks of killer whales, he found himself adrift within 60 seconds with his family of five to "claw a place for themselves in the savage ecology of the Pacific Ocean." On taking inventory, he found his wife's "sewing basket was a treasure beyond wealth" because of its fantastic contents. Survive the Savage Sea, (c) 1973 Praeger Publishers, Inc., New York, Dougal Robertson.

Your survival kit, instructions for raft repair, contents of pockets, contents of raft pockets, and personal belongings should be examined. One lifeboat was once sailed for weeks using a minute compass found on the watch chain of one of the crew. Expect corrosion rapidly to affect your watch and any metal instruments. Within a few days, Petty Officer Dixon found his automatic pistol to be a solid rusty mass which he used later as a hammer. You can clean the metal with oil or grease or fat from any bird you catch but invariably the salt water corrosion catches up with you.

What signaling gear do you have? You may be lucky. In 1937, George Claude advised the French Air Force that dye could be spread as a marker on the sea; the French ignored his suggestion but the Luftwaffe didn't and adopted his idea with benefit since the North Sea and the English Channel were the grave of many a wartime pilot. Yet by 1965, dye cartridges and smoke grenades still were not standard items for civilian lifeboats. Got a mirror? Radar chaff? Flares? What about a whistle and a working flashlight? Yes, thank God, here they are.

HEALTH

Seasickness is an invariable companion for a few days. Half the crew of rafts will be seasick within eight hours and will need three days to get their sea legs. The old sailor's advice is of no help: "One sure cure for seasickness: go and sit under a tree." Unfortunately, sharks will be attracted to the vomitus and will eat it. The misery of the castaways is compounded by the constant banging noise of the sea on the floor of the raft. Survival stories are full of this complaint, "like Chinese torture." The vomiting compounds the dehydration and electrolyte imbalance castaways have and can lead to fits of fury and delirium with irrational behavior. Supplies and food have been flung overboard in those confused states which compare with the irresponsible odd behaviors in scuba diving "rapture of the deep," and the anoxic situations of mountain altitude sickness when climbers will throw away or forget their gloves, as mountaineer Maurice Herzog did on Annapurna and as happened to pilot Guillaumet in the Andes. The problem of dehydration and vomiting is so well understood now and so recognized by parents that it was not uncommon for me seeing small children with this complica-

tion in Texas to find the mother already had a suitcase packed in anticipation that I would be hospitalizing the child.

The skin also suffers. It is difficult, even impossible, to keep dry, and soggy waterlogged skin has little resistance to infection. This is the basis for "salt water boils," which are described by almost every person who has been adrift on the open sea. The skin peels, then becomes infected. The lips crack and even engine oil is of no value in lubricating them, although animal fat helps, as it does in the rectum also for constipation. "The sun is like Hellfire." The eyes are dazzled. The skin never tans; it simply burns, peels, then burns and peels again. The eyes redden. Teeth rot. Hair crusts and scratches become most painful. Defecation is tiring due to the constipation and in weakened state, many have fallen overboard from the raft. I paint such a picture, it is a wonder Errol Flynn ever was able to attract pretty women onto his raft — oh, sorry, he had a yacht not a raft.

The skin changes are partly due to the vitamin deficiency, especially of Vitamin C, but mostly the effect of exposure and salt water. Most seaplane operators hose down their aircraft every night with fresh water after use in salt water because they have learned the lesson now being demonstrated to the castaway in the raft. Sea water rapidly rots clothing; zippers rust, guns and watches rust, canned food cans corrode and lose their contents. Fresh fruit and vegetables rapidly rot. Nor does rain necessarily improve the situation. After the exhilaration of fresh water washing and drinking comes the chill of the storm. The fingers can be so numb with cold that they cannot inflate the raft or even loosen a collar and tie. The thrashing of the rain stings like hot needles and the trauma can cause the body to swell and become stiff.

The will to live is decreased by those thermal stresses. Heat, cold, wind and injuries can make malnourished castaways too tired to paddle towards food drops, too exhausted to bail a sinking lifeboat, too weak even to climb back on board if they have fallen off the raft. Hear them: Madden, one survivor at sea, "too weak to pump" and another, Twining, "too tired to paddle," and poor Ericsson, "too cold to row." I recall once when I was in the Parachute Regiment talking to a sergeant who had been in a disastrous battle at Arnhem when the Allied Airborne were dropped in vain to reach the Rhine before the bridge was blown. He said, "Bullets were dropping all around us but we were just too tired to care."

Weakened members of the crew can actually slump into the bottom of the raft and be drowned by overcrowding. There are about 170 bathtub drownings a year in the United States and a baby can drown in a cupful of water by similar mechanisms. Changing position is painful, difficult and at times liable to overturn the raft. Leg cramps are common and there are blood changes, e.g. of calcium which are similar to those affecting astronauts in space.

The will to live is important. Troebst feels that civilized man has lost his sixth sense "which protects primitives." Instincts and premonitions are lost. Wilfred Noyce in his study of the will to live, *They Survived,* (c) 1963 E.P. Dutton & Company, Inc., New York, goes back to the Russian physiologist Pavlov and his work with dogs. Pavlov noted four basic types of dog: the "strong excitatory," the "weak inhibitory," the "lively" and the "calm imperturbable." He also noticed that more concentrated and severe stress could be applied to the two latter groups before they broke than the first two. Noyce feels that survivors tend to come from similar latter groups in humans. Certainly in the plane crash of the football team in the Andes, the leaders came from tough groups similar to those described by Pavlov. In other words, it is the old maxim "trust in God in the storm, but keep on paddling."

But it's not quite as easy or glib as that. Training cannot change your character or personality but it sure can change your chances of survival. Trained groups whose life styles or careers bring them into disaster perform more efficiently under stress than others. "Panic among miners is rare." Police, firemen, doctors, priests, even former Boy Scouts cope with duress better because of the benefit of their former training.

Troebst points out that people often survive the disaster to succumb to the aftermath. He points out that 2700 United States men (38% of captives) died in captivity in the Korean War. This is a higher percentage than of all the American soldiers who died in captivity from the time of the Civil War to 1952. Troebst feels that this was not due to bad treatment by the enemy but that soft civilian-soldiers could not cope with despair, resignation, privation and fear. A common complaint of the military was "we were taught how to fight, but not how to survive."

You *can* learn how to survive — many have done it the hard way and some have learned it for others. A French surgeon, Alain Bombard, stated in 1951 that of the 200,000 who die at sea every year, (my God! that number's got to be wrong!), 50,000 die from lack of survival training. He worked in the port of Boulogne where there were 100 - 150 drownings annually. He decided to prove that man could live from the sea (later Thor Heyerdahl would say "to starve to death was impossible"). On 25 May 1952, Bombard and a friend, Jack Palmer, left Monte Carlo in a 15 foot by 6 foot rubber raft, reaching Tangier when Palmer left. Bombard departed Tangier 13 August and left the Canary Islands 19 October 1952. He then sailed 3750 miles to St. Lucia, Barbados on a voyage lasting 65 days in the open sea. He lived on raw dolphins and birds, and caught flying fish. He drank one pint of salt water daily (see subsequent discussion on this). He lost 55 pounds in weight, developed anemia, diarrhea, lost his toenails, had a severe itch and skin rash and had defects in vision. In his account, *The Bombard Story,* (c) 1954, Simon &

Schuster, Bombard says, "It was not a question of living well, but of surviving long enough. I got there."

Poor Bombard, the brave and courageous step he took to prove a point had only a brief impact and a decade later, the Navies of many countries were still ignoring the lessons he had demonstrated. Bombard's weight loss was not unusual. In 1953, a Finn Ensio Tiira, age 24, accompanied by a Swede, Fred Ericsson, age 23, decided to jump ship in the Straits of Malacca off Sumatra. They were in the French Foreign Legion en route to the war in Indochina. Ericsson was fastidious and would not eat raw fish and died of exposure. The winds blew their raft westward into the Indian Ocean. When finally picked up after 32 days, Tiira had lost one third of his normal weight from 132 pounds, and five days after rescue, weighed only 56 pounds! *Raft of Despair*, Ensio Tiira, (c) 1954, Dutton, New York.

WATER

Okay. Let's talk about the most important factor of all. Sea survival without water: maximum 11 days. Fear of dying of thirst is the constant torment of the castaway. Coleridge said, "Water, water, everywhere, Nor any drop to drink." Was he right? Yes. Let me be emphatic because there are so many conflicting authorities and so many theories in print. There is an inescapable fact: TO EXCRETE THE SALT IN ONE PINT OF SEA WATER, YOU NEED MORE URINE THAN THE WATER CONTAINED IN THE ORIGINAL PINT. Flight Lieutenant John Smith was shot down in July 1943 near Munda in the Pacific. He believed he survived due to eating bird fat (he shot birds) and two pints of salt water a day. His physicians felt he survived because, just prior to the crash, he had taken a heavy fresh water intake and also had rain on the fifth day. It is now known that drinking urine, salt water or alcohol does not help the castaway. The American, William Willis,

who crossed 6700 miles of the Pacific in a raft in 1954 felt like Bombard that there was a place for salt in the diet, but Doctor Hans Lindemann, who has crossed the South Atlantic three times since 1957 in small boats, disagrees. He found in raw fish that only the eyes, the blood and the fin fluid were salt free. He felt you could tear out the pocket from your pants, put in a piece of fish and chew the pocket for juices and that you would do well "since fish lymph is low in salt" but United States authorities disagree and say that even this is too salty.

Castaways in their thirst suffer mirages, false hopes, delusions and hallucinations. They sneak salt water, by mouth washing and "accidentally" swallow some. Doctor MacDonald Critchley describing shipwreck survivors: "When a thirst-crazed castaway drinks salt water . . . the victim becomes quiet and apathetic, with a strange fixed and glassy expression in his eyes . . . delirium sets in . . . consciousness disappears . . . froth appears at the corners of the mouth . . . death comes quietly . . ."

Death does not always come quietly. When the German training ship Pamir sank in September 1957 during a hurricane, two cadets drank sea water and delirious by next day, jumped overboard. The British Board of Trade has a November 1965 Merchant Shipping Notice #M.500 which states very emphatically "Seafarers are reminded that if castaway they should never under any circumstances drink sea water."

If you anticipate a rain storm, wash down your raft and your clothes in sea water to remove the heavy crust of salt on them, wash down the floor of the raft then dry it, then as the first rain hits, keep rinsing your clothes until they are soaked finally with fresh water. You can then squeeze out the clothes into any suitable container. Again, your Saran Wrap bags used previously as floats can be used as water containers. If you are collecting in a sail or tarpaulin, the first lot off the canvas will be quite brackish.

FOOD

Bombard felt food was all around him. Fairfax was followed across the Atlantic as he rowed Britannia by a shoal of dolphin which gave him a constant supply of fish. He would feed parts of a fish caught to the others to keep them happy and staying faithfully in attendance. The monotony of his food stores so offended Fairfax that he threw some supplies overboard. Robin Knox-Johnson, the first man to sail nonstop around the world solo (1968-69), found his food supplies so boring and tedious that he arrived back home 11 months later with a three months' supply of canned goods still present.

Your first supply of food will be fish. Line fishing may be out of the question as the shark may take any struggling fish on your line — and your line also before you know what's happening. A gaff is the answer. Keep parts of fish not eaten as bait. By feeding your fish in attendance, they may be contented enough to stay put when you go for them with any hook device or even your hands. Due to phosphorescence, your fish may normally fluoresce in the dark — this does not mean that the fish is spoiling. Fish have been caught by firing guns under water to stun them. Always open the belly of a large fish for the extra benefit of small fish which may be contained therein. Fish lines have been made from laces, and threads from seams of clothing. Fish hooks have been fabricated from fish and bird bones, pocket knives, shoe nails, needles, pins and even pencil clips. Survivors have eaten barnacles from the bottom of the raft, algae, and the small crustaceans found in floating rotten logs.

In *Lost Ships and Lonely Seas,* (c) 1921, The Century Company, author Ralph Paine tells of the brig Polly which left Boston in December 1811 to be disabled completely in a gale, drifting for an incredible six months in the Atlantic before the last two survivors were rescued near the Canary Islands. They were becalmed for weeks in the dreaded Sargasso Sea but found it "beneficent. The stagnant weed swarmed with fish and gaudy crabs and mollusks."

"Harvest the sea," cried Alain Gerveault who as far back as 1923 sailed from Gibralter to New York. His method of collection of plankton, a minute form of sea life, was duplicated by the Kon Tiki expedition. Heyerdahl used a funnel-shaped 18 inch diameter net with 3000 meshes to the square inch. Several pounds of plankton porridge were collected every few hours, foul smelling but edible. This is very nutritious and in fact, the blue whale lives on it. Don't confuse plankton with tiny, minute jellyfish which sting and are painful to swallow, and in fact, check your puree for jelly and jellyfish which you should remove. Sometimes you can catch plankton only at night and sometimes never. The net can be improvised from clothing.

Flying fish are manna from Heaven. They will often remain in an area long enough for you to paddle the raft to them when some will fall into your vessel. You can sometimes rig up a sheet cloth or sail and shine a light on it at night or turn it to the moon when flying fish may jump onto it.

Castaways usually gut the fish, then string them up or lay them out to dry in the sun. In general, fish in the open sea are edible, although poisonous fish are sometimes found near land.

"Poisonous fish generally look very ugly, with deep set eyes, a small mouth like a parrot's beak, slimy gills, a ball- or box-shaped body, hard scales, dangerous looking prickles, or loose whitish skin. Their ventral fins are stunted or completely missing. Their flesh often has a repulsive odor, and if you press on it, the dent remains for some time, as it does if you press on the legs of people suffering from leprosy or dropsy." *The Art of Survival,* (c) 1965 Doubleday & Company, New York, Cord Christian Troebst.

Turtles as a food are well-described in Dougal Robertson's two books; his second being *Sea Survival — A Manual,*

(c) 1975 Praeger, New York. Turtles are killed with difficulty by shooting them in the head or slitting the tough skin around the neck when the blood also can be drunk.

Birds will, at times, settle on your raft — especially after a storm when they will be exhausted. Try to be patient and wait until they fold their wings before grabbing. The former United States athlete Louis Zamperini survived 47 days in the Pacific living on "albatross birds, fishes and the liver of a shark."

Cannibalism has apparently been more common than realized. The Andes crash of 1972 reminds us of the Donner Party which was trapped in the Sierra of California in 1846 and which also resorted to that expediency.

The American whaler Essex lost in the Atlantic in the 19th century also saw cannibalism amongst the crew.

SHARKS

Long before the book and movie *Jaws* rocked the nation, there were the shark stories, if you knew where to look for them. The horror of the survivors' anecdotes is enhanced when you remember that dead men tell no tales. Those who claim that shark attacks are rare fail to appreciate that the statistics apply only to where we know the details. The mind boggles at the unknown, and the flesh creeps at what the true figures might be.

It can be predicted that sharks are unpredictable. There are 250 species and what applies to one does not apply to another. However, in August 1960 a shipwreck at the mouth of the Komati River in Mozambique saw only three survivors out of 49 after a shark attack. When the S.S. Nova Scotia sank off South Africa, more than 1000 died from shark attack. The ship Indianapolis suffered dreadfully from shark attack although apparently there was some exaggeration in the movie *Jaws*. In August 1826 when the Magpie sank instantly in a squall in Cuban waters, 15

sharks initially played with the men swimming alongside their longboat until one man lost a leg, with instant frenzy and mass attack. Within an hour, there were only two survivors.

There are about 15 Americans attacked each year on United States beaches. It will be a slight comfort when drifting on the open sea to know that the worst shark attack in the U.S.A. occurred 20 miles upstream in a New Jersey creek. I tell patients in the office that the lab test available to detect occult hidden blood in bowel movement is so sensitive that it detects one part blood in one million parts stool. A merchant sailor then gravely told me that sharks can detect one part in six million.

Blood is a lure so don't swim with dead fish speared by you hanging from your belt and don't swim if you have bleeding cuts or are menstruating. Swim quietly without vibrations, which to the shark's radar resemble the thrashing around of a fish in distress. Swim in company as 80% of shark attacks are on solo swimmers at least ten feet away from other swimmers. Some sharks seem to attack white skin and leave alone or avoid dark clothing, which may be a good reason for keeping your pants on. Sharks have been punched off, clubbed off with gun butts and oars, shot off with signal flares and smoke grenades. Some decaying fish were found to be avoided by sharks and were thought to be rich in ammonia acetate. This formed the basis where crystals of copper acetate were used as a shark repellent with some success.

It is said that *some* low frequency sounds repel sharks. "Great," someone said, "all you have to do is make the correct low frequency sounds and try to avoid making the low frequency sounds which attract sharks!"

In the meantime, remember the snout of the shark is sensitive. It can be hit on the nose or poked in the eyes. The tow bar is a useful tool for this, which is why you grabbed it from the plane.

Harold Corbett, who was rescued by a

fishing boat 1 January 1978 off Hawaii, after ditching his light plane, said he spent 15 hours of the New Year kicking off sharks nibbling at his feet.

LONELINESS

This is a common problem and all stories are full of sadness when the autobiography of any sea survivor discusses the death of the last comrade and the writer is left on his own. Singing is said to help and even nonreligious people fall back on prayer. Many have independently referred to the strange sensation they have of a Presence on the raft as if they were not alone. This apparently gives great comfort.

NAUTICAL SKILLS

A rubber raft sits high on the water and its walls act like sails. The raft will skim along at times before the wind and your progress like an airplane may be a composite of current and wind. Pride of seamanship comes through in some of the survival adventures; some castaways refused to drift. They kept logs and rough maps. Dixon and his two younger pilots paddled with shoes opposite the current and put down a homemade sea anchor when the wind was unfavorable. Tiira made a sail out of a shirt and two oars for his direction. Robertson knew exactly where he and his crew of five had to go to reach the shipping lanes. None of those drifted aimlessly. Man's great endurance: in 1896, two Norwegians, Harbo and Samuelson, rowed 3000 miles in 55 days from Manhattan to England.

Some nautical skill is required should you not be picked up at sea and should you have to bring your raft in for a landing. Obviously, you would choose a beach rather than rocks. If you have no choice, go for the rocks where the water slides up them, not where it bangs with a great spurt of spray. Have everything on the raft tied down, you may still need the raft contents even when on land. Remember, tired swimmers can fall on the beach and drown in shallow water. The first person swimming to shore should try to get bearings on the others. Take a sight on a person still in the water and scratch an arrow or line in the sand towards him. Then run down the beach about 30 to 50 yards and take a second angle and mark the sand to get a cross bearing. Keep looking at the person in the water until he is in shallow water and safe.

If you are being dashed against rocks, reverse in the water and lead with your feet. If your shoes have lasted this far, this is a good time to have them on. In the dreadful wreck of the Killarney in Ireland in January 1838, 43 survivors were finally driven by the waves onto the rocks on the shore. Only 13 were saved, and all through the storm that night could be heard the shrieks as yet another slipped from his hold into the sea. The moral is: You mustn't quit too soon, never give up, you are not home yet. It is similar to the situation described by Don Downie, "A tail dragger really isn't through flying until it's been pushed into a hangar, chocked, and the hangar door shut — and locked!"

If on the other hand you are being picked up by a boat in a storm or heaving sea, try to get a line thrown to you as the boat in the swell can be a dangerous weapon. Let the boat come to you — don't tire yourself swimming to it.

Well, will you all make it? You have survived a ditching, found your raft and maintained your health on the open sea. Will you survive? Of course, you will make it. Poon Lim made it and so will you. He was a Chinese sailor shipwrecked when the SS Ben Lomond was sunk by a U-boat in 1942 in the South Atlantic. He found an empty lifeboat with food and water for 25 men. He made the water last 50 days, then lived on rain, seaweed, fish and plankton. He was rescued by a Brazilian fishing boat after a record incredible 133 days in the open sea.

What does it take to fly successfully over water? Is it really different from other terrain flying? Perhaps the answers are not found from study of the successful flights but in analysis of the failures.

Let us question the United States Coast Guard Air Station at Miami — the world's largest air-sea rescue unit and so busily engaged at the time of my visit that there were five separate rescue missions being flown. They have around 700 emergencies a year with about 20% involving aircraft.

"What can general aviation pilots do to minimize problems over water and to facilitate help should they need it?" I asked. "Well, you wouldn't make a motor bike trip without a helmet," they replied, "so why fly over water without a life-jacket!" Yet apparently this is what is done. A recent four plane Cessna accident spotlighted errors made by untrained, unprofessional pilots. The engine started to run rough 20 miles from the Florida coast; instead of nursing it and trying all combinations of power, mixture richness, carburetor heat and single magneto running, the pilot apparently shut down the engine and ditched. There were only three life-jackets for four people and in the water

after a commendable ditching, the group decided to split up since they thought, wrongly, that four separate targets had a greater chance of being spotted from the air than the assembly of four.

A recent high performance Beech single engine aircraft accident was also on their minds. The pilot was too proud to say he was lost and communicated with the Coast Guard only when he was down to twenty minutes' fuel. He was four hours from any possible rescue unit but an American Airlines jet was generous enough to come down from 35,000 feet to 1500 feet in an attempt to see and pinpoint the location of any splash as the aircraft ditched. The plane sank immediately, however, with all three occupants drowning.

The Coast Guard often suspects that the inexperienced water flyer is so unrehearsed in his emergency skills that he loses the precious altitude required for radio communication while ponderous mechanical attempts are being made to restart an engine. LTJG Robert Ausness, who is also a CFI, states, "The most important object in an over water flight sur-

A position report or estimate can make the vital difference between a successful rescue and a failure. There's a lot of open ocean around our shores; let your Mayday contain your position.

Photo Credit: E. G. Anderson

A welcome sight if it comes before you freeze. A HC 130 B on ice patrol. Photo Credit: U.S. Coast Guard

vival kit is the plane radio — use it early."

We're kinda back to the old FSS 5 C s again with climb and communicate hitting priority #1.

The tale continues: sixplace Pipers laden — yea overladen with six burly Midwest students and their load of camping gear heading for the Bahamas and, over gross, disappearing forever; the planes zigzagging from cloud shadow to cloud shadow low on fuel with the original heading lost and forgotten; the Bellanca taking off VFR and attempting to fly around a thunderstorm, forgetting how widespread those storms can be at sea, and never returning. Bellanca — what an insult to a man and a plane which in 1927 had the greatest potential for being first across the Atlantic to Paris, and which failed to achieve this distinction only because of personality clashes in its crew.

And then the Mooney which ditched with all the lifejackets and survival gear under the suitcases in the baggage compartment. Hell, you buy a Mooney for speed and sacrifice cabin room. "Can you imagine four people attempting to get lifejackets out with their engine failure at 1500 feet MSL altitude. Can you just imagine the agony and confusion?" the Coast Guard asked me in anguish at man's stupidity. The only thing that saved this group was that magnificent floating Mooney wing.

The Coast Guard also sees, too frequently, the rental family crowding into the rented Piper and confronted with choice of lifejackets and/or life raft save a buck in rental costs by making for them the ultimate wrong decision. The tales go on.

LTJG Penn Shade demonstrated to me on the Coast Guard wall charts just how extensive the ocean is and in their situation, how the four knot Gulf Stream current can have a man in the ocean 50 miles from any ditching within 12 hours. Penn, who comes by coincidence from Pennsylvania, a State proud of its reputation for aviation safety, feels that the basic old proven value of filing a flight

152

plan and sticking to it is often forgotten by the pilot flying the outdoors. Penn brings to his own flying over water the awareness of a possible engine failure any time a plane is in the air. Always know your ditch heading the way over land you are always aware of surface wind and possible emergency landing sites, is his message. As part of his constant scan when he flies his Coast Guard helicopter or his private light plane over terrain, is his next constantly updated emergency landing spot . . . "I fly from field to field," he smiles modestly, and you get a flash of the true professional.

Bob Chamberlain, the son of a Pan Am airline pilot and himself a CFII with several thousand hours of flying time in the East Florida area, comes across also as the seasoned professional pilot. He feels that in general aviation, indifferent navigation and poor fuel management have been the major causes of over water disasters. "You must know your point of no return, your distance to land and how long your fuel will last." His finger stabs a wall chart at Pro Air Opa Locka Airport. "For instance, if I'm over water here and my fuel is this much, then I know immediately that in 63 minutes I'm going to be wet."

We'd better get smart. It's preparation, rehearsal and being aware. You can't really practice ditching. Maybe we'll have to redefine a successful landing as one you walk away from or swim away from. As the Coast Guard says, "Better listen to us, 'cause we're the ones that fish you out!"

I wonder if they had heard of John Berryman's prayer: "Lord have mercy on my son: for he is a lunatic and sore vexed: for ofttimes he falleth into the fire, and oft into the water."

You made it. Aren't you glad the Feds made you carry a raft?   *Photo Credit: FAA Aviation News*

11
THE
SAFE PILOT

"O wad some pow'r the giftie gie us
To see oursels as ithers see us!"
ROBERT BURNS

AND SOME
PSYCHOLOGICAL
ASPECTS OF
FLYING

THE SAFE PILOT AND SOME PSYCHOLOGICAL
ASPECTS OF FLYING

Statistics show that the neophyte with 100-300 hours flying time is over-confident about his skills and frequently appears in accident figures. Unfortunately, his pride literally comes before a fall; the average pilot does not fly for very long before he meets a problem his flight instructors did not tell him about — sort of like "things you always wanted to know about flying but were afraid to ask."

As his hours increase, so does his humility until, again, at about 3000 hours his bold self-reliant assurance returns to give another peak in accident statistics As the Department of Transportation points out, how about saving a life this year, like maybe your own — "charity begins at home." James Rudolph, Director of Flight Standards for the FAA, states that the safe pilot has "three things going for him: an aptitude for flying, experience and knowledge." The training and certification programs (to a degree) remove those with little aptitude; but we have to look to ourselves for the other two factors.

George K. Dorn, aviation safety specialist with the active Pennsylvania Bureau of Aviation, a most thoughtful organization that has done much for the prevention of aviation accidents, points out three failings of man which make him appear in flying accidents.

Firstly, man tends to esteem more his willingness to take a chance than to be cautious. Certainly, we all tend to brag more of our misadventures in the air than to boast of the mundane.

Secondly, we tend to rationalize our actions, as children do. We justify buying an airplane, any new possession, changing an occupation, location or anything which touches our life as if we had done it by logic rather than by emotion. Thus we often make a decision because we want

to, although we try and usually succeed in feeling that it was done as the best objective consideration. "Destination fixation" falls into this category of error.

Thirdly, the Pennsylvania accident analyses show that "men will risk losses out of all proportion to possible gains if they feel that through their skill and luck, they can probably avoid the loss." Why? If we really knew, there would be no history, no epics and no marathons in life. Again, I think we are back to the need for experience and knowledge; we have to search out our own "soft spots" and be self-critical, be as it were our own check pilots. It will take years to see if the Biennial Flight Reviews and the "Safety Pin" programs have achieved results, but the initial impression is that they have.

I recall my "Safety Pin" check with Demi Copadis, a New England Accident Prevention Specialist. He soon revealed that he expected professional performance the goal of any pilot. Knowing that errors in preflight preparation and planning account for 17% of general aviation accidents, I had been thorough with the preflight check. Later, Demi muttered, "Heck, doc, your preflight was almost a fetish, but I thought you'd have enough pride to taxi on the yellow line."

I have found occasional dual instruction of great value and especially before any long vacation trip if I haven't flown much recently. It is now well known that total hours is not so important as recent hours and how current the pilot is.

Before heading off to fly the outdoors, the pilot would do well to "put his house in order" and this means simulated practiced emergencies with an abrasive, persistent, determined instructor in the right seat. Perhaps initially, in a simulator, the outdoor pilot could have hammered into him procedures for fires in flight and electrical and vacuum failures. Then he should be put through the mill at altitude. A door should be popped on him in flight, a takeoff should be aborted on rotation and a skilled instructor should be able to bring his pilot to a sharpness which will enable him to land on an adjacent runway with an engine pulled a few hundred feet above the runway. Learn at altitude the numbers for your aircraft and study the erudite scholarly treatise by Barry Schiff "to turn or not to turn" in the magazines *Flying* and *Pilot.*

Again, at altitude, over an airfield, stop your propeller and make a real dead stick landing with tower permission and with help from the right seat. You should learn the difference between glide with a windmilling prop and a dead prop in practice with an instructor present and not as a real event with your family aboard and screams rending the air (the screams coming from the left seat, I mean). If not IFR rated, you should again review the aircraft manual procedures and practice your 180's and recoveries from unusual altitudes. When did you last give yourself 60 seconds on the turn and bank instrument? If a VFR pilot, your CFI should arrange an instrument flight in IFR weather; the first time you are immersed in a wet cloud should not be in illegal conflict with the F.A.R.'s when you are solo and non IFR rated.

Your instructor should turn off the fuel tap so often (ever had that done to you at the top of a chandelle?) that it becomes fast second nature for you to check fuel any time your engine falters. You should also get some experience flying from the right seat; again, the first time you try to judge your flare from the right seat should not be with a gasping, frothing figure in the left seat. Such seating will allow your check pilot to manipulate surreptitiously the contact breakers or fuses for further simulated emergencies. We don't practice enough, and it does make a difference. In fact, it is pretty clear that planes are better than pilots. As the FAA says, there is, however, a limit to the airplane, "it

can't bore holes through a mountain or fly with empty tanks."

Experience and knowledge as part of your baggage are the easiest of all your accoutrements to carry around with you, and do make for better pilots. However, as Harold Brown, M.D., Director of Safety and Education of the Flying Physicians Association, points out, better pilots are also improved by proper rest before flying, and by avoiding stress in allowing adequate time for preparing the flight and preflighting the aircraft. He points out the value of getting the spouse or co-pilot to attend to passengers and baggage to avoid distractions for the pilot. Bon voyage parties are to be avoided and you should probably try to get to bed early your first day out even though jet lag as we know it does not occur in light plane flights.

In flight, the pilot should use his knowledge and experience to give him objective awareness as to how the flight is progressing. In general, pilots refuse to act early when things go wrong, and keep hoping that they have more options than they really do. Decisions are delayed in the hope that a decision won't have to be made and an early precautionary landing in daylight with power on is turned into a vertigo spin with fuel exhaustion in darkness. In a survey of 898 accidents, 60 were the result of the landing being on unsuitable terrain with one fatality; whereas 46 were due to continued VFR into IFR with spatial disorientation involving 33 fatalities. Obviously, the precautionary early landing is a lot safer than delaying for the inevitable final curtain but pilots are loathe to damage aircraft in order to protect themselves. When Hurricanes and Spitfires were shot down over England during the Battle of Britain, important though the aircraft were, it was the salvage of their even more precious pilots that turned the tide for Britain. People are more important than things, or as W.L. Taylor says, "Bend some aluminum rather than break a neck." Read any author-pilot of the 1920-

1930's. They were always making precautionary landings and doing them well. True, engines and planes are now more dependable but that doesn't mean you must never be skilled in forced landings or ignore the need to sharpen another skill.

There are several practical things a pilot can remember in his forced landing concepts.

He can make a point of using shoulder harnesses as well as seat belts. Ignore all the twits who, well meaning, cite fire, unconsciousness, and "saved by accidental ejection in the crash" as factors why they never buckle up. The Los Angeles Police Department on their freeways have demonstrated the value of seat restraints, and any ambulance driver, emergency squad or emergency room crew have similar thoughts.

Secondly, remember your mathematics. IF you can cut your landing speed by say two, you can reduce the total destructive energy force by a factor of 4. Your emergency landing speed, therefore, is always just above stall but at minimum controllable speed.

Thirdly, an engine cooled by a glide with fuel taps off is seldom going to ignite on forced landing.

Fourthly, learn with a sharp instructor (and hopefully in a rented plane and not your own!) your own personal limits of skill in landing. Practice the tricks of spot landings. You can stretch a glide sometimes by diving into ground effect to increase your airspeed and lengthen your float in ground effect. This is the opposite instinct to what the student pilot would do. If you are too high on your approach and cannot turn or slip, you can retract your flaps back from full to zero, then back immediately to full which is guaranteed to lose you height. If in the float you are sailing too far in ground effect, you can wiggle your wings abruptly which will disturb the airflow so much that you'll drop out of the float. Tricks like this are no substitute for sound conventional flying but there may be times when practiced safely with a sound instructor, they make the difference between landing safely or not.

You see, R. L. Stevenson was not always correct when he said "to travel hopefully is a better thing than to arrive."

EPILOG

"Come my friends; 'tis not too late

to seek a newer world"
Tennyson

"Life is a journey

not a destination"
Anon

"Every journey must have a soul"

Anon

"You started out nervous and excited—like a virgin.
You went in fat and came out lean. You made it."
Albert Saijo

"You ramble home. What happened? Nothing."
William Strafford

"You listen badly and you read even worse.
Except when the talk or the book is about yourself."
Dag Hammarskjold

APPENDIX

RADIO DATA

VHF RECEPTION DISTANCES

Line of sight with no terrain obstructions

Plane Altitude AGL Feet	Reception Distance in Statute Miles
1000	45
3000	80
5000	100
10,000	140

ATIS SEQUENCE

Code Letter: Ceiling: Visibility: Wind: Temperature: Dew Point: Altimeter: Approach: Runway: Notam

POSITION REPORT

ACFT Ident: Position: Time: Alt: IFR/VFR: Est. Next Fix: Name Succeeding Fix: Pireps

PIREPS

Report Conditions Aloft - Cloud tops, Bases, Layers, Visibility, Turbulence, Haze, Ice, Thunderstorms

TIME TO STATION

$$\frac{60}{\text{Degrees Flown}} \times \frac{\text{Time Flown}}{} = \frac{\text{Time to Station}}{}$$

MAYDAY SEQUENCE

"Mayday Mayday Mayday
ACFT Ident x 3
Type ACFT
Position, Heading, Airspeed
Altitude
Fuel Remaining
Nature of Distress
Intentions
Assistance Desired
10 Second Dash Mike Button x 2
ACFT Ident x 1
Over"

TRANSPONDER CODES

0000	Never Use
1200	VFR
4000	Restricted & Warning Areas
7600	Lost Comm.
7700	Emergency

Radiotelegraph Code and Phonetic Alphabet International (ICAO)

Letter	Phonetic	Code		Letter	Phonetic	Code		Letter	Phonetic	Code
A	Alfa	·—		M	Mike	——		Y	Yankee	—·——
B	Bravo	—···		N	November	—·		Z	Zulu	——··
C	Charlie	—·—·		O	Oscar	———		0	ZE-RO	—————
D	Delta	—··		P	Papa	·——·		1	WUN	·————
E	Echo	·		Q	Quebec	——·—		2	TOO	··———
F	Foxtrot	··—·		R	Romeo	·—·		3	TREE	···——
G	Golf	——·		S	Sierra	···		4	FOW-er	····—
H	Hotel	····		T	Tango	—		5	FIFE	·····
I	India	··		U	Uniform	··—		6	SIX	—····
J	Juliett	·———		V	Victor	···—		7	SEV-en	——···
K	Kilo	—·—		W	Whiskey	·——		8	AIT	———··
L	Lima	·—··		X	Xray	—··—		9	NIN-er	————·

WEATHER

Meteorology

Height of low clouds	Ground level to 6,500 feet
Height of middle clouds	6,500 to 16,500 feet
Height of high clouds	Bases 16,500 to 45,000 feet
Temperature difference from standard equal to one per cent altimeter error	5 degrees F.

TERM	VALUE
Normal lapse rate	2 degrees C per 1,000 feet 3.5 degrees F per 1,000 feet
Lapse rate to determine altitude at which clouds will form in vertically moving air	4.5 degrees F per 1,000 feet
U.S. Standard Atmosphere Barometric pressure Altimeter setting Temperature	 1013.2 mb 29.92 inches Hg 59 degrees F 15 degrees C
Moist adiabatic lapse rate	2 degrees F - 5 degrees F
Air flow around low pressure area	Counterclockwise
Air flow around high pressure area	Clockwise
Altitude to which surface friction slows wind	1,500 to 2,000 feet

AVIATION WEATHER REPORTS

SKY AND CEILING

Sky cover symbols are in ascending order. Figures preceding symbols are heights in hundreds of feet above station.

Sky cover symbols are:

○   Clear: Less than 0.1 sky cover.

◐   Scattered: 0.1 to less than 0.6 sky cover.

◍   Broken: 0.6 to 0.9 sky cover.

⊕   Overcast: More than 0.9 sky cover.

—   Thin (when prefixed to the above symbols)

—X   Partial Obscuration: 0.1 to less than 1.0 sky hidden by precipitation or obstruction to vision (bases at surface).

X   Obscuration: 1.0 sky hidden by precipitation or obstruction to vision (bases at surface).

WEATHER AND OBSTRUCTION TO VISION SYMBOLS

A	Hail	IF	Ice Fog
AP	Small Hail	K	Smoke
BD	Blowing Dust	L	Drizzle
BN	Blowing Sand	R	Rain
BS	Blowing Snow	RW	Rain Showers
D	Dust	S	Snow
E	Sleet	SG	Snow Grains
EW	Sleet Showers	SP	Snow Pellets
F	Fog	SW	Snow Showers
GF	Ground Fog	T	Thunderstorms
H	Haze	ZL	Freezing Drizzle
IC	Ice Crystals	ZR	Freezing Rain

WEATHER, CONTINUED

WEATHER SYMBOLS

S⟶	Sandstorm or Snowstorm
≡	Fog
,	Drizzle
•	Rain
✳	Snow
△	Showers
▽	Hail
⌐↘	Thunderstorm
⌇	Smoke
∞	Haze

WIND SPEED

PLOTTED	Miles (Statute) Per Hour	Knots	PLOTTED	Miles (Statute) Per Hour	Knots
⊙	Calm	Calm		44-49	38-42
	1-4	1-2		50-54	43-47
	5-8	3-7		55-60	48-52
	9-14	8-12		61-66	53-57
	15-20	13-17		67-71	58-62
	21-25	18-22		72-77	63-67
	26-31	23-27		78-83	68-72
	32-37	28-32		84-89	73-77
	38-43	33-37		119-123	103-107

Wind speeds as plotted on surface weather maps

164

DEPICTION OF FRONTS ON SURFACE WEATHER MAPS

TYPE	IN BLACK AND WHITE
Cold Front	
Warm Front	
Occluded Front	
Upper Cold	
Upper Warm	
Stationary	
Squall Line	

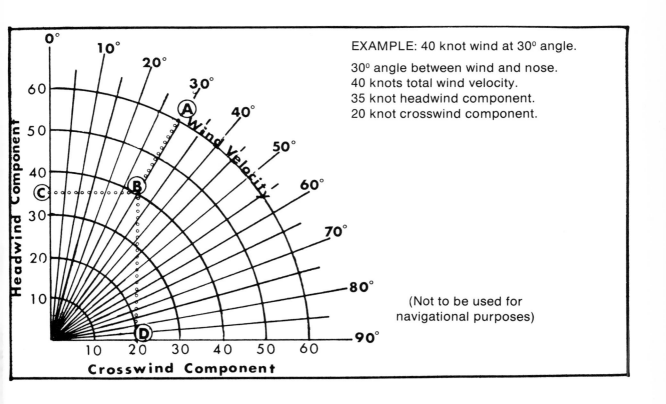

EXAMPLE: 40 knot wind at 30° angle.

30° angle between wind and nose.
40 knots total wind velocity.
35 knot headwind component.
20 knot crosswind component.

(Not to be used for navigational purposes)

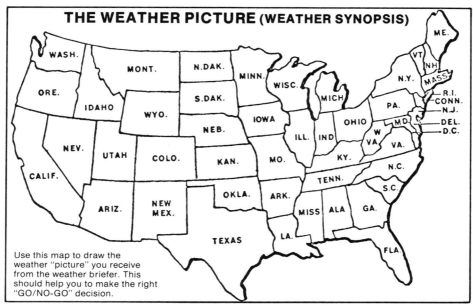

THE WEATHER PICTURE (WEATHER SYNOPSIS)

Use this map to draw the weather "picture" you receive from the weather briefer. This should help you to make the right "GO/NO-GO" decision.

Use the space below to jot down the weather data as you receive it.

EN ROUTE WEATHER		DESTINATION WEATHER	
LOCATION	**REPORTED**	**LOCATION**	**REPORTED**
		/////////	**FORECAST**
/////////	**FORECAST**		
			NOTAMS/SPECIAL INFO

WINDS ALOFT		HAZARDOUS WEATHER	
LOCATION	**FORECAST**	**LOCATION**	**TYPE**
SURFACE WINDS			

EMERGENCY PROCEDURES
GROUND-AIR VISUAL CODE FOR USE BY SURVIVORS

Require Doctor Serious Injuries	I	Require Signal Lamp with Battery and Radio	I I	Require Fuel and Oil	L
Require Medical Supplies	II	Indicate Direction to Proceed	K	All Well	LL
Unable to Proceed	X	Am Proceeding in this Direction	↑	No	N
Require Food and Water	F	Will Attempt Takeoff	▷	Yes	Y
Require Firearms and Ammunition	⋁	Aircraft Seriously Damaged	⊐	Not Understood	⌐L
Require Map and Compass	□	Probably Safe to Land Here	△	Require Mechanic	W

If in doubt, use International Symbol   SOS

INSTRUCTIONS:

1. Lay out symbols by using strips of fabric or parachutes, pieces of wood, stones or any available material.

2. Provide as much color contrast as possible between material used for symbols and background against which symbols are exposed.

3. Symbols should be at least 10 feet high or larger. Care should be taken to lay out symbols exactly as shown.

4. In addition to using symbols, every effort is to be made to attract attention by means of radio, flares, smoke or other available means.

5. On snow-covered ground, signals can be made by dragging, shoveling or tramping. Depressed areas forming symbols will appear black from the air.

6. Pilot should acknowledge message by rocking wings from side to side.

AIRPORT OPERATIONS
HAND SIGNALS

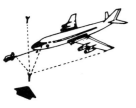

SIGNALMAN DIRECTS TOWING

SIGNALMAN'S POSITION

FLAGMAN DIRECTS PILOT TO SIGNALMAN IF TRAFFIC CONDITIONS REQUIRE

ALL CLEAR (O.K.)

POINT TO ENGINE TO BE STARTED

START ENGINE

PULL CHOCKS

COME AHEAD

LEFT TURN

RIGHT TURN

SLOW DOWN

STOP

INSERT CHOCKS

CUT ENGINES

NIGHT OPERATION

EMERGENCY STOP

GROUND-AIR VISUAL CODE FOR USE BY GROUND SEARCH PARTIES

No.	MESSAGE	CODE SYMBOL
1	Operation completed.	L L L
2	We have found all personnel.	L L
3	We have found only some personnel.	++
4	We are not able to continue. Returning to base.	X X
5	Have divided into two groups. Each proceeding in direction indicated.	⇄
6	Information received that aircraft is in this direction.	→
7	Nothing found. Will continue search.	N N

NOTE: These visual signals have been accepted for international use and appear in Annex 12 to the Convention on International Civil Aviation.

Body Signals

**Need mechanical help
or parts — long delay**

Negative (no)

Affirmative (yes)

**Land here (point in
direction of landing)**

**Do not attempt
to land here**

All OK, do not wait

**Our receiver
is operating**

**Pick us up —
plane abandoned**

**Can proceed shortly,
wait if practicable**

Use drop message

**Need medical
assistance, URGENT**

AFTER
AOPA

HOW TO USE THEM

If you are forced down and are able to attract the attention of the pilot of a rescue airplane, the body signals illustrated on this page can be used to transmit messages to him as he circles over your location.

Stand in the open when you make the signals. Be sure that the background, as seen from the air, is not confusing. Go through the motions slowly and repeat each signal until you are positive that the pilot understands you.

FLIGHT PLANNING

APPROXIMATE LOCATIONS OF ISOGONIC LINES IN THE UNITED STATES

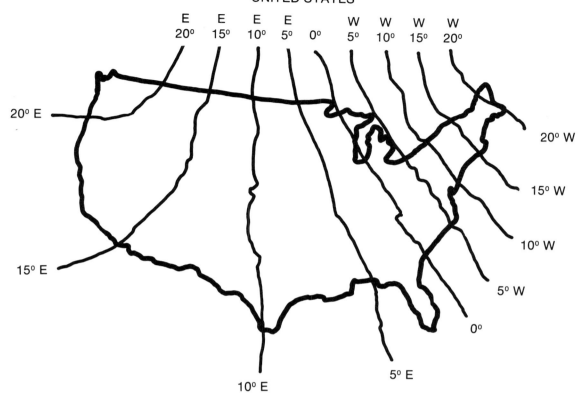

VFR Altitudes/Flight Levels
Controlled and Uncontrolled Airspace

Courses are Magnetic

Under VFR—More than 3,000 feet above the surface.

Below 18,000 feet

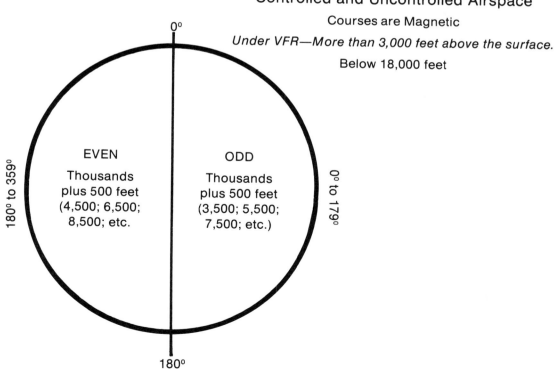

GASOLINE OCTANE	FUEL COLOR
80/87	Red
100/130	Green
100/130 low lead	Blue
115/145	Purple

ROTATING GROUND BEACONS

12 to 15 per minute for beacons marking airports, landmarks, and points on Federal airways.

12 to 40 per minute for hazard beacons.

COLOR

The color combinations of rotating beacons and auxiliary lights are basically:

White and Green	Lighted land airport
*Green alone	Lighted land airport
White and Yellow	Lighted water airport
*Yellow alone	Lighted water airport
White and Red	Landmark or navigational point.
White alone	Unlighted land airport (rare installation)
Red alone	Hazard

*Green alone or yellow alone is used only in connection with a not far distant white-and-green or white-and-yellow beacon display, respectively.

VASI LIGHTS

Standard FAA 2-bar VASI

(a) Below glide path	Red	Runway	Red	
	Red		Red	
(b) On glide path	Red	Runway	Red	
	White		White	
(c) Above glide path	White	Runway	White	
	White		White	

LIGHT GUN SIGNALS

Color and Type of Signal	On the Ground	In Flight
STEADY GREEN	Cleared for takeoff	Cleared to land
FLASHING GREEN	Cleared to taxi	Return for landing (to be followed by steady green at the proper time)
STEADY RED	Stop	Give way to other aircraft and continue circling.
FLASHING RED	Taxi clear of landing area now in use (runway)	Airport unsafe. Do not land.
FLASHING WHITE	Return to starting point on the airport	
ALTERNATING RED AND GREEN	General warning signal — exercise extreme caution	

TIME
Standard to GMT

Eastern	+ 5 hours	= GMT
Central	+ 6 hours	= GMT
Mountain	+ 7 hours	= GMT
Pacific	+ 8 hours	= GMT
Yukon	+ 9 hours	= GMT
Alaskan	+10 hours	= GMT
Bering	+11 hours	= GMT

Add one less hour for Daylight time.

FLIGHT PLAN SEQUENCE

Type flight plan	Remarks
Plane number	Est. time en route
Plane type	Fuel (hours/minutes)
Est. TAS	Alternate airport
Point of departure	Pilot's name
Proposed dep. time	Pilot's address
Cruising altitude(s)	No. persons aboard
Route	Plane color
Destination	

BASIC AIRCRAFT CHECK LIST

Before starting engine
- ☐ Preflight aircraft
- ☐ Safety belt on
- ☐ Parking brake - as required
- ☐ Controls - free
- ☐ Carburetor air - cold (off)
- ☐ Propeller - HI RPM
- ☐ Mixture - full rich
- ☐ Fuel - on - check quantity
- ☐ Landing gear - DN. Position
- ☐ Electric switches - check
- ☐ Cowl flaps - open (if appro)
- ☐ Clear propeller
- ☐ Master switch (bat & gen) on
- ☐ Ignition switch - on both
- ☐ Start engine (ref. A'C'FT man)
- ☐ Check oil pressure

Before landing
- ☐ Gas (fuel) proper tank(s)
- ☐ Landing gear - down
- ☐ Mixture - full rich
- ☐ Propeller - HI RPM
- ☐ Aux fuel pump (on if appro)
- ☐ Carburetor air - as required
- ☐ Flaps - as required
- ☐ Trim - as required

Before takeoff
- ☐ Brakes - check on taxi
- ☐ Instruments - check/set
- ☐ Fuel - proper tank(s)
- ☐ Trim tab(s) - takeoff pos'n
- ☐ Propeller check
  - ☐ Exercise
  - ☐ Set - HI RPM
- ☐ Engine check
  - ☐ Oil - press & temp
  - ☐ Carb air (for ice)
  - ☐ Magnetos - check
- ☐ Carburetor air - cold (off)
- ☐ Flaps - as required
- ☐ Step - up (if appro)
- ☐ Controls - operate & check vis.
- ☐ Windows & Doors - check
- ☐ Clear runway & area

After landing
- ☐ Flaps - up (clear of runway)
- ☐ Cowls flaps - open (if appro)
- ☐ Propeller - HI RPM
- ☐ Stop engine mixt. full lean
- ☐ Ignition switch - off
- ☐ Electric switches - all off
- ☐ Parking brake - on (if required)

CHECKLISTS - BASIC EMERGENCIES

CRASH LANDING:

Mayday
Master off
Fuel off
Land gear up usually

DITCHING CHECK LIST

Preflight:

ELT
Life jackets
Raft
Flares Smoke
Survival Kit
Rope

Flight:

Radio contact
Weather
Wind direction and strength
DITCH HEADING
Spot surface ships

DITCHING:

Convert speed to altitude
Trim best glide
Emergency check list
Stow gear
Lighten plane
Practice removing shoulder belt
Remove glasses, sharp objects, etc.
Wedge door open
Power-on-slow-behind-power-curve
Nose high 10 - 12 degrees
Wait till plane stops
Get out FAST

CHECKLISTS - BASIC EMERGENCIES

ENGINE FIRE:

Turn fuel off
Mayday
Give position and land

COMPLETE POWER LOSS:

Switch fuel tanks
Boost pump on
Full carburetor heat
Mixture rich
Mag check
Primer locked
Ignition on
Master switch on

SMOKE IN CABIN:

Master switch off
Cabin heat off
Ventilate cabin

ELECTRICAL POWER LOSS:

Master switch off
All electrical switches off
Use battery for emergency tasks,
    then turn off again

LANDING GEAR MALFUNCTION:

Lower wheels with emergency system
Switches off at ground roll

NATIONAL OFFICES
OF OTHER AGENCIES

Forest Service
U.S. Department of Agriculture
Washington, D.C. 20250

Bureau of Sport Fisheries and Wildlife
U.S. Department of the Interior
Washington, D.C. 20240

Bureau of Reclamation
U.S. Department of the Interior
Washington, D.C. 20240

National Park Service
U.S. Department of the Interior
Washington, D.C. 20240

Bureau of Indian Affairs
U.S. Department of the Interior
Washington, D.C. 20240

FLYING FAMILY PLAN. The author with his four co-pilots loads up.

Photo Credit: Charles L. Cashin, Jr.